TIME PAST TO TIME FUTURE

The church – my past experience and future hopes

Douglas Rhymes

Foreword by Simon Phipps

DARTON · LONGMAN + TODD

First published in 1993 by
Darton, Longman and Todd Ltd
1 Spencer Court
140–142 Wandsworth High Street
London SW18 4JJ

ISBN 0–232–51944–7

A catalogue record for this book is available
from the British Library

Unless otherwise stated, most biblical quotations
are taken from the New English Bible
© 1970 Oxford and Cambridge University Presses

Phototypeset by Intype, London
Printed and bound in Great Britain at
the University Press, Cambridge

TIME PAST TO TIME FUTURE

For all the clergy and laity
with whom I have worked in ministry
over the last fifty years

CONTENTS

Part Three: Looking to the Future

FOREWORD

Douglas Rhymes is exceptionally well qualified to write this book. A parish priest to his finger-tips, he has served in down-town and mid-town and suburban country parishes and as an army chaplain. A long-standing and vocal member of the General Synod, he has also held the important appointment of director of lay training for the Diocese of Southwark. Few people, with the residentiary canonry attached to that work, have then positively chosen to return to work in a parish, and in an inner-city parish at that. Few have then taken all that experience to a commuter village, where he established a businessmen's study group, which has continued after his retirement for over ten years. Now he is 'on supply' in the Sussex countryside and lectures on ethics at a theological college. He is indeed qualified to look at the future of the church on the basis of what he has seen of its past.

His book will appeal to those who see the church as a means to the Kingdom and not as an end in itself. The words 'reality' and 'creativity' mean for him being serious about 'what is', and perceptive and responsible about what may be. The book is both pastoral and prophetic. Pastoral care and counselling, marriage and divorce, sexuality and homosexuality, pastoral spirituality and the nature of community all receive fresh and radical thinking – as do the environment in terms of creation, the ordination of women, the relationship of clergy and laity in the Body of Christ and the future of worship in a post-Christian culture. The importance of appropriate training for Christians in all these things underlies the whole.

This is a book of clear integrity, coming, as it does, from one who has lived out, in sustained action, the implications of what he has come to believe.

SIMON PHIPPS
former Bishop of Lincoln and
Chairman, Industrial Committee of the Board for
Social Responsibility of the Church of England

PREFACE

'The end is where we start from' – these words by T. S. Eliot from 'Little Gidding'[1] sum up the whole intention and purpose of this book. In December 1991 I celebrated fifty years of pastoral ministry as a priest in the Church of England. I now look back on that ministry, but not with nostalgia. To do that would be entirely negative and I certainly would not expect anyone to waste their time simply reading of my past experiences. The only healthy way for me to look back is to be able, from the experiences both personal and ministerial, to look forward to the future. So the end is where I start from. I am not writing an autobiography. I am simply using what I have learned and experienced as a guide to reflection on the future needs and changes in the thinking and structure of the Church of England, if that church is ever to speak again with reality to the mass of the people.

I have recently been reading Kenneth Leech's book *Care and Conflict*,[2] and I could echo his words: 'What I am offering – all I can offer – is personal experiential theology.' But his experience has been different from mine, both as a person and in the situations of ministry. He speaks mainly from a ministry almost entirely in inner London. I speak from a ministry almost evenly balanced between inner city and outer suburbs, so that perhaps we may complement each other in our vision for the future of our church.

When I speak of personal experiential theology I am again speaking of two different kinds of experience: that which comes from a gradually increasing and deepening knowledge of myself and that which comes to me from the situations in which I find myself and the people with whom at various times I am involved in those situations.

I shall also be aware that since theology is concerned with reality – ultimate reality – I must try to speak from the objective reality of both myself and the situation. Both of these are difficult, since my perception of myself may well be clouded by the way I want to see myself and the way I want society to see me, and my interpretation of the situation may also be far from the truth in that phrase often used today: 'real terms'. In trying to see myself as I am, I shall therefore need some kind of assessment of what is reality which will also be appropriate to any theological thinking arising from it. Again, if the situation is to be viewed theologically – that is, with the mind of God as seen through Christ – then this can only be done if the situation itself is realistically assessed. Moltmann offers a valuable way of doing this:

> The church always belongs within the context of the world, whether it likes it or not. This means that it is quite simply essential for the church, every minister and every congregation to see themselves as far as possible in context, and to become involved, with all their minds and capacities, in the conditions, powers and potentialities of the society they are living in. But the context is not the text, and we must never allow it to become so. The church's context is society. But the text is the Gospel of Jesus Christ.[3]

I would like to add how greatly I have been helped over fifty years of ministry by all who have worked with me in the various parishes as clergy and lay colleagues. I have learned much from them and we have equally endured much from each other! I cannot single out all who have been of great help, but there are a few to whom I owe a special debt of gratitude: Dr Cecilia Goodenough and Bishop John Robinson, from whom I learned that new understanding of contextual theology which has dominated my thinking ever since; Frank Edwards, who from his own experience as a business executive strongly supported my attempts at Woldingham to link theology with business ethics and stress, and contributed greatly to the continuity and value of the Business and Professional Group founded there; Canon Eric James, who as my spiritual director encouraged me to write this book; also Bishop Simon Phipps, who talked over with me the plan of the book, encouraged me in the writing of it, and wrote the foreword; and John Clark, who since Camberwell days has combined warm and deep friendship with perceptive and often valuable criticism of both me and the church. Finally I am deeply grateful to Jill Johnston, my co-partner in leadership of the Pastoral Support Group in Chichester, who undertook to type my erratic typing more readably on her word processor – a truly mammoth task which I am sure she must often have regretted undertaking, but has never said so!

DOUGLAS RHYMES
Fontwell, West Sussex

April 1993

1 T. S. Eliot, 'Little Gidding', *Four Quartets*, Faber 1944.
2 Kenneth Leech, *Care and Conflict*, Darton, Longman and Todd 1990.
3 Jurgen Moltmann, *Christian* (vol. 6, no. 5, Epiphany 1982), p. 81.

Part One

REALITY AND CONTEXT – PAST EXPERIENCE

1

BACKGROUND TO MINISTRY

First it is necessary to describe briefly and as honestly as I can the reality and context of my life up to the beginning of my ministry, leaving the experiential theology which has arisen from those facts to be more fully worked out later.

Although I was born in Devon just before the beginning of the First World War, most of my early life was spent in Birmingham where my father was a mathematics master at a local grammar school. I was an only child; there should have been a sister when I was about four years old but my mother had a miscarriage. My home was the reasonably comfortable and conventional home of an average middle-class family of that between-the-wars period. In my early childhood, while my father was away in the war, and after-wards in training, I spent a great deal of my time with my mother and grandparents. My religious upbringing there-fore alternated between the somewhat dull, matins-type religion of the average Devon country church when I stayed with my paternal grandfather (very much the strict Victorian master in his own household!) and the more rigid, but to me equally dull, non-liturgical worship of the Plymouth Brethren, which was the religion of my maternal grand-parents. (Sunday there was more or less continuous chapel with nothing permitted that was 'not suitable' for the Sabbath.) I remember as a boy saying that the only reason I preferred the Anglican Church to that of the Brethren was because with a liturgical service I knew at least when it was coming to an end! All my grandparents were very much in the Victorian mould, in the sense that nothing was ever discussed in front of me that was considered socially or sexually taboo. I am convinced, as was Philip Larkin,[1] that

3

parents, without meaning to, can have a damaging effect upon the development of personality, and I am quite sure that my father's somewhat detached emotional personality and my mother's very possessive attitude towards me all through my life, especially after the death of my father, had a great influence on my own sexual orientation.

As I grew up I discovered that my feelings towards women differed from those of most of my friends. I was friendly with many girls and always enjoyed their company, as I still do (in fact in terms of friendship I often prefer women's company), but I felt very little sexual attraction towards them. This I regarded as strange and a cause of deep regret because I knew instinctively, as a matter of reality, that this would mean that I should not marry and have children, which I would have liked to do.

In those days I did not think of myself as homosexual or 'gay' (that word had not yet been invented as a description of homosexuality), because people did not talk in those terms – not because they were more tolerant but rather because they were more ignorant of the whole subject. In some ways life for the unmarried was easier in those days because no insinuations were made – two men or two women living together were not automatically stamped as gays or lesbians but were seen simply as friends who chose to live together. Perhaps sometimes 'where ignorance is bliss 'tis folly to be wise'!

This reality I discovered about myself did not cause me to feel guilty or a sinner, but it did give me a sad feeling that life would have been more complete and less difficult if marriage and family had been my lot and I would not have had to pretend whenever anyone said to me, 'What a shame you have not found the right girl yet!' I did not feel sinful when sometimes I experienced strong love for my male friends, even in a physical sense, because I saw this as like the love of David for Jonathan, described by David himself as 'passing the love of women', and this I felt had always been approved of by the church. It was only later I discovered that somehow the church made a distinction between that historic love in the Old Testament and the love relationship of two men today. Anyway, so much for the personal back-

4

ground which explains why I have always felt the need to support and speak for a more understanding and creative attitude towards all minorities.

Returning to my religious affiliations, despite my boredom with the forms of religious worship offered me as a boy, both at home and at school, this did not lead me away from the church but rather to be increasingly critical within it. In the same way, while I have always found myself at odds with the values and conventions of middle-class society, I remain very definitely middle-class in my style of life. (Probably one of the weaknesses of the Church of England is that both in training and ministry it is more at home with the middle class than with any other grouping because most of the clergy are middle-class, either by background or by educating themselves above their background.) We cannot avoid the reality of what we are, but let us recognise that many of our opinions and values arise from what we are rather than from any specifically Christian ethic. By the touchstone of that reality which in this book I am seeking, I must regard myself as a dissatisfied insider religiously and socially rather than a rebellious outsider. What I think we have to avoid is being complacent and satisfied insiders as so many have become in the last twenty years.

During the period leading up to the Second World War I found myself in new areas of thinking both religious and political. I was introduced by a friend to one of the leading Anglo-Catholic churches in Birmingham, St Jude's, Hurst Street (now demolished). Here I found a form of worship conveying a transcendence, mystery and beauty of symbolism which made an immediate appeal to me and has continued to do so. I also found there a preaching and teaching which firmly linked theology and social need – especially from the curate, who later became Bishop of Bradford.

These were the days of Baldwin and Chamberlain, when political conservatism seemed incapable of realising the threat of Hitler or of arousing any enthusiasm in a young man. I was at that time at Birmingham University mixing regularly with lively and intelligent socialists like Louis Mac-Neice, Ron Willets, Stephen Spender and often W. H. Auden (we met each week to discuss politics in a pub outside the university). To me, real opposition to Hitler necessitated the unity of all left-wing groups, and for a time I joined the Communist Party – later, of course, to be betrayed by communism. Those days left me with two attitudes to politics which have remained: first a strong feeling that despite its weaknesses the Left is likely to be more concerned with the poor and hence the Kingdom of God than the Right: secondly a profound cynicism about politicians and their lack of moral consistency.

After a period in the insurance profession I had felt increasingly drawn towards the Anglican ministry. The testing of my vocation was very strange: it consisted of two interviews, one with Bishop Barnes (then Bishop of Birmingham) in which I listened for about half an hour to a lecture on religion and science and said practically nothing myself. (I now say that I cannot be worried by so-called heretic bishops since I was confirmed and interviewed for ordination by Barnes, worked for years with John Robinson and sat on a theological education committee for some time with David Jenkins!)

The other interview was by the Diocesan Ordination Committee, who seemed mainly concerned with my lack of interest in cricket and wondered if anyone could be ordained who didn't like cricket! Whatever people may say about the present selection process, it is at least far more thorough in interviewing potential candidates than the system before 1939.

Trying to get business for an insurance company taught me much of what is necessary if one is to get others interested in religion: that you need to study the person you are trying to influence, be aware of the technique of approach most likely to succeed, and not be over-pushing but rather keep alongside. A course in selling insurance might well be a valuable asset to evangelism! I well remember that when I told the manager of the office where I worked that I was leaving insurance to train for the ministry he replied: 'Well, it will not be greatly different – you will be selling people what is very good for them but they are often reluctant to see it.'

It was then I went to Birmingham University, where I

chose to read philosophy for my degree. I had already begun to realise that truth is reached by search and questioning rather than by acceptance of dogma, and it seemed to me that philosophy would raise the questions before theology began to give the answers. Later, of course, I realised that theology did not give the answers but only raised different questions. I took my degree in July 1939, an ominous time. I had intended to go to Oriel College, Oxford, to take a degree in theology but in September the war started. Although I was in a reserved occupation I did not feel justified in spending time taking a second degree, so I chose to go straight to theological college in order to be ordained as quickly as possible and later serve as an army chaplain. Here I experienced the wide variety of thinking within the Church of England. Ripon Hall, Oxford was a college which, while liberal modernist in its emphasis, had students of every shade of both ecclesiastical and political opinion. Ian Ramsey, later Bishop of Durham, was a fellow student and even at that stage his open and logically reasoning mind had a great influence on me.

1 Philip Larkin, 'This Be the Verse', *Collected Poems*, Faber 1988.

2

EARLY DAYS AND THE WAR

I was ordained in Chelmsford Cathedral in December 1940 as deacon and as priest in the following year. For two and a half years I served in the east-coast parish of Dovercourt, where earlier searching had led me to feel I would be working with a vicar with whom I would have affinity, trust and confidence. Here in an area where invasion was seen as a high risk I had a mixed experience as curate of the parish, chaplain to various army and air force units, member of the Home Guard (which truly was 'Dad's Army' in both equipment and training but nevertheless had a wonderful sense of community and purpose) and air-raid warden. It was good training for my next step, which was to volunteer for army chaplaincy in 1943. Eventually I found myself posted to the 30th Armoured Brigade, the only brigade of flail tanks in the British Army and destined for the task of blowing up mines preceding infantry attacks when the invasion of Europe took place in June 1944. I remained with this brigade, and particularly with the regiment with whom I lived (the Westminster Dragoons) until after the ending of the war in Germany. Owing to the nature of the task we were either at the very front of action or well away in relative safety until next required, and I had every opportunity of testing the truth of the old saying that 'war is ninety per cent boredom and ten per cent hell' and of ministering in both circumstances. (Since life appears to be like that for many people this was a very valuable experience!) Despite the horrors of war I found this period in many ways the most satisfying of my whole ministry – for three reasons.

First, I have never been so identified with those whom I served as I was in the army. I was living the same life and sharing the same dangers and feelings in a way which has never been true in civilian life. Normally one of the difficulties of being a clergyman is that you sense a great gap between your life and that of most of your parishioners. In that situation the stereotype given you emphasises the gap, but it was not so in the army. The officers in the brigade were a very mixed group and included a film star, Ian Carmichael, the future chairman of the Olympics, Lord Killanin, a future leading barrister in income tax law and a future headmaster of Bradfield and Harrow public schools. The 'other ranks', who were also from different professions and areas of industrial and business life, treated me as a valuable link between civilian life and the army, since by inclination I saw my work as much more pastoral than official and was treated accordingly. Later I came to see that it was this same matter of identification that often made the non-stipendiary priest who shared priesthood with a secular occupation, or the local priest who came from the same group and area where he exercised his priesthood, more effective than those who came straight into ministry from school and university.

Secondly, my army service taught me how much could be achieved if one got alongside people, how little if one did not. I found this to be true also of my fellow officers – the more they demanded that they should be treated as superior the less they received respect. This again I have discovered in the hierarchy of the church; some bishops seem to behave as though they were superior beings whose ideas should be accepted by all within their dioceses or they distance themselves from their clergy in such a way that the behaviour of the clergy becomes either an obsequious desire to please or a fearful submissiveness. In such cases there may be external obedience but there is little true love and confidence.

Thirdly, I learnt that what is called 'folk religion' is never to be despised. There are many levels of approach to the spiritual and some are far more instinctive than reasoned. In the army, where fear of the unpredictable is closely linked with anxiety about what is happening to relationships at home, but where there is a strong sense of community with one's fellows rarely experienced in civilian life, there will be many mixed motives and reasons for coming to worship or to prayer or discussion with the padre which would never take place in civilian life. If one can learn to accept people where they are rather than where we want them to be, much valuable help and teaching can be given which may well have results in later life. I used to make a practice of giving copies of the addresses given at army services to those present, and after many years I met someone who told me that he had still retained some of them. I had felt some amusement that the office which typed my sermons would always send 'copy to colonel, copy to adjutant' – I hope there also they did some good!

3

SOUTHWARK DAYS

The experience which changed my whole theological thinking and has remained as the motivation for all future search and study came some years after the war. I returned from the army to serve as a priest in Romford, Essex, and there I had my first experience of ministry in a large council housing estate. From there I had a short period in Chelmsford and then I crossed the River Thames to the Southwark Diocese in south London, where I was to spend the rest of my ministry until retirement. Here I had the interesting combination of being a minor canon and sacrist of Southwark Cathedral and also priest-in-charge of a back-street parish with a once famous Anglo-Catholic church (now bombed) behind the Borough underground station.

This was very much the area described by Charles Dickens, and in many respects it had changed little from that period. There was a squalor in which it was no uncommon experience when visiting to step aside on the stone stairs in a block of flats to allow a rat to shoot by, and one often had to keep a wary eye on the bugs crawling up the walls. Yet there was among the people a sharpness of wit and a cheerfulness of neighbourly spirit so characteristic of the south Londoner. I learned, both from the council estate and from the Borough, how flexible methods of worship and preaching need to be and of the limitations which our fixed liturgy and theological training put upon such necessary adaptability. Churchmanship there had very little to do with doctrine but much more to do with how people wanted to express themselves; in a drab neighbourhood being 'high church' simply meant a natural desire to have colour, movement and rhythmic music. Vestments, incense and choruses to hymns

11

spoke much more to natural feelings than to any particular Catholic doctrine. Preaching meant learning how to articulate the faith in the simplest way and not to expect more than limited understanding. Theological colleges seem never to have learnt a way of training the clergy so as to enable them to preach to people who read the *Sun* or the *People* rather than the *Telegraph* or the *Independent*. This may partly explain why the churches in suburban areas always draw larger congregations than those in inner-city areas.

In 1954 I became vicar of New Eltham, in what I would call a 'middle middle-class' area, with mostly semi-detached houses. The congregation were a reasonably young articulate group who were neither at the top nor the bottom of the work ladder. In terms of church membership this was the most successful parish in which I have served. I had three excellent curates, many efficient and keen lay leaders and a parish in which there was little secular community organisation. As a result, the church had every opportunity, and used it, to become very much the centre of community life in the area. I think probably it is still true that the church with the best chance of being effective in its area is one having an articulate and enthusiastic laity, who are not over-pressurised with executive responsibility in their work and therefore have time and capacity to devote to other activities. In New Eltham I began to see that lay leadership did not mean just leadership within the local church, but had a role in promoting the 'text of Jesus Christ in the context of society' and in interpreting the Gospel in secular work situations and in local and national politics. The following passage by Ruth Etchells, which many years later was adopted in the report on *A Strategy for the Church's Ministry*, had already seemed to make obvious sense to me:

> To be called to lay service is to be called to live fully in the secular world, to be at ease in it, to know its idioms and assumptions, to engage in its arguments and affairs, because one's centre is there. It is not to sally out from one's real centre, the parish church and its affairs, or the diocesan structures, for sorties into industry or trade or education or politics or whatever. It is to live in

industry or trade or politics, to earn one's income from them; to be committed to them: and there, in that place where one's energies are committed, to engage quite consciously in mission and ministry. It is to see oneself as committed for work outside the 'club' of the church.[1]

I had therefore set up study groups in the parish with case studies from the experiences in every-day secular working life of my parishioners and their problems in order to help them relate their Christian thinking and action to their secular responsibilities. These were well received and found valuable in the wider area of all the churches.

As a result of this I was asked by the Bishop of Southwark, Mervyn Stockwood – at the instigation of John Robinson, Bishop of Woolwich – to be the first director of lay training in the diocese and warden of the diocesan training centre, Wychcroft, a large house in Surrey. As a base for the work I was made a residentiary canon of the cathedral.

This was an exciting period for the diocese of Southwark. Already Bishop Stockwood had become a controversial figure for his left-wing political views, and then his suffragan, John Robinson, was to outdo him in controversy and provoke thousands of people to take a new look at theology when in 1963, shortly after my appointment, he published *Honest to God*.[2] This book quickly became more of a bestseller than any other theological book for generations.

Why did this book have such an effect? In actual fact Robinson was simply trying to reshape crude but all too common thinking about God – namely, the supra-naturalistic idea that God was some sort of super-object 'out there', if not 'up there'. As he himself wrote in a notable article in the *Observer*, 'It is our image of God that must go'. Kenneth Leech commented on this:

> The god whose image must go might well have been a caricature of the Christian God, but it was a caricature which corresponded with a widely held view, a view which effectively prevented any real engagement with God as a living reality. Robinson did not create this situation: he merely laid bare the reality of existing confusion and unbelief.[3]

But he did more than this, and that was the reason for the excitement caused by this book. He revealed the incapacity of the church to communicate truth as truth, choosing rather to hide behind a credal orthodoxy which must not be questioned lest the whole fabric of the church disintegrate. He liberated many of us, including myself, to be able to view truth as a continuing search which has no limit, rather than as a casing of dogma within which we must always remain. The questioning which began for me at university and continued in the forces was now, as it were, permitted.

I found it possible to retain the roots of my eucharistic catholic upbringing, since that now spelt out for me the communal background and interrelationship of all life: 'Just as this eucharistic action is the pattern of all Christian action, the sharing of this bread the sign of the sharing of all bread, this fellowship is the germ of all society renewed in Christ.'[4] And I was able to join this with an inquiring and non-dogmatic approach to all thinking, whether religious or political or social. (Perhaps, as John Robinson once said, this is the true meaning of 'radical' – one who reaches out from roots.)

I said at the beginning of this section that this experience changed my whole thinking and has remained with me ever since. It has caused me to be profoundly critical and even antagonistic to the present polarisations in religious thinking between fundamentalist evangelicalism on the one hand and dogmatic traditional catholicism on the other.

In politics also, and for the same reasons, I find myself looking with suspicion at both Thatcherism and the extreme right on the one hand and the militant extreme left on the other, since both seem to find satisfaction in thinking that they alone have the truth. Nevertheless, I believe that no one who takes seriously the 'text' in the 'context' can stand outside religious or political organisations. Since the kingdom of God is concerned with all areas of life, my past and present experience leads me towards what is called 'liberation theology' as that which seeks to link Christ's message of liberation (Luke 4:18) with active political responsibility for the poor, the oppressed and the captive.

My experience then of the *Honest to God* days, and what was called by opponents 'Southbank religion', led me to the conclusion that in the search for truth the consciousness of uncertainty is a better guide than dogma. The purpose of faith is more likely to be found in enabling one to live with insecurity than in unquestioned acceptance of credal orthodoxy. I began to realise the wisdom of the words of Kahlil Gibran:

> Say not, 'I have found the truth,' but rather, 'I have
>   found a truth.'
> Say not, 'I have found the path of the soul.'
> Say rather, 'I have met the soul walking upon my path.'
> For the soul walks upon all paths.[5]

It was during this period that I wrote two books. These were sparked off by the thinking of *Honest to God* and were entitled *No New Morality*,[6] (a defence of the so-called new morality which was really based upon situation ethics, and *Prayer in the Secular City*,[7] which developed the theme of prayer as a praying of life rather than a saying of prayers. Kenneth Leech described accurately what I was seeking to do in that book:

> In 1967 Douglas Rhymes in an important book, *Prayer in the Secular City*, a study which is still valuable today, attempted to develop Robinson's ideas in relation to the prayer life of modern man, defining prayer as 'the in-Christness which lights up all our actions in daily living from within'.[8]

My very gently liberal book on morality caused at the time a great deal of controversy. For several weeks there were letters in the *Church Times* protesting at the sermons in Southwark Cathedral on which the book was based. Mervyn Stockwood describes in his autobiography *Chanctonbury Ring* how seventy evangelicals demanded to see him to discuss not only my book but also *Honest to God* and the refusal of another canon of the cathedral, Canon Pearce-Higgins, to give public assent to the Thirty-nine Articles. Bishop Stockwood rightly said that my intention in *No New Morality* was to 're-think the Church's attitude towards sex', and that my basic contention was 'the need to reverence human personality and not to isolate the sex act'. Yet as Stockwood somewhat amusingly put it: 'Unfortunately the word "sex" is to many churchmen what a red rag is to a bull. Social injustice, apartheid, nuclear warfare, economic exploitation, slums, illiteracy were trivial ills as compared with the horrors of "bed".'[9]

The ideas in my book would raise few eyebrows today; like John Robinson's views they have now been widely accepted, but the temptation to rush in with protest to every new slant in theological or moral thinking is very strong in the church. Very few heed the words of Gamaliel:

> 'Leave [these men] alone. For if this idea of theirs or its execution is of human origin, it will collapse; but if it is from God, you will never be able to put them down, and you risk finding yourselves at war with God.' (Acts 5:38–9)

1 From an article by Ruth Etchells, quoted in the Tiller Report, *A Strategy for the Church's Ministry*, General Synod 1983.
2 John Robinson, *Honest to God*, SCM Press 1963.
3 Kenneth Leech, *True God* (Sheldon Press 1985), p. 6.
4 John Robinson, *On Being the Church in the World* (SCM Press 1974), p. 71.
5 Kahlil Gibran, *The Prophet* (Heinemann 1926), p. 66.
6 Douglas Rhymes, *No New Morality*, Constable 1964.
7 Douglas Rhymes, *Prayer in the Secular City*, Lutterworth 1967.
8 Kenneth Leech, *Soul Friend* (Sheldon Press 1977), p. 30.
9 Mervyn Stockwood, *Chanctonbury Ring* (Sheldon Press 1982), pp. 152–3.

4

LAY AND CLERGY TRAINING

The work and post of director of lay training to which I was appointed was new to the diocese. Most of my fellow clergy and laity seemed to think that lay ministry was assistance for the clergy in running the parochial organisation. As John Betjeman put it: 'For P.C.C.s were really made/To give your local vicar aid'. Sadly, I find that, even after thirty years in which lay training has become more widely known, this is still the view generally held, at least in the parts of Sussex where I now live.

I came to the work with a conviction that the priority for the whole people of God is to be engaged in mission to the world and not just to the church, but how this was to be expressed in training, and whether my view was shared by lay people in the parishes, I had only a general idea. It seemed sensible that a lay person of experience both in theology and in working amongst the laity should be associated with me in this work and I asked Dr Cecilia Goodenough to be my colleague. There could have been no one better suited – as the daughter of an admiral who had lived a good deal of her life in the inner city and had worked with industrial mission, the homeless and one-parent families, she had first-hand experience and was also a theologian of distinction.

Together we decided that our first job must be to find out what the laity themselves wanted from lay training. The diocesan conference house, Wychcroft, was used as a training centre for the Southwark Ordination Course, a course of training started by John Robinson and Canon Stanley Evans for men who combined daily work in the world with ordination training through evening classes and weekends of residence. We decided to use the weekends not required by the ordination course to gather together groups of lay people from all parts of the diocese; sometimes we had groups from the inner city and sometimes from suburbia or the higher levels of management in what was often called 'the gin and Jaguar belt'. We asked these groups what they felt they needed as training to be Christians in a secular world. Most of them said the same, that the difficulty lay in relating Christian thinking and action to a technological and complex world far different from the world of first-century Palestine: the text was the same but the context was very different. They pointed out that Christ used examples from the world around him – shepherds, tax-gatherers, fishermen, agricultural labourers – to illustrate his teaching. How then could we illustrate that teaching in a world of computer analysts, nuclear technicians, stockbrokers, scientists, modern farmers, executive managers, trades unionists, advertisers, programme planners in TV and radio, and journalists? They complained that the clergy saw them only in relation to their role in the local church and not in their Monday-to-Friday life where most of their witness as Christians was to be seen. I remember one man saying with a mixture of irony and exasperation: 'My vicar last week introduced me to someone as his "head server". I thought of my daily work as managing director of a firm where I was responsible for the lives and future of over ten thousand people. It had never occurred to me that my most important witness as a Christian was likely to be on Sunday mornings as head server!'

As a result we designed weekends of training where scriptural study and theological thinking were linked to case studies of daily work and personal accountability. These studies were supplied in some cases by participants from their own experience, others came from our own knowledge of parochial and industrial or social life. Sometimes we would gather together a group of people from the same work or cultural background, so that they could share their experiences and work out a common ethical responsibility. Sometimes we quite deliberately mixed a group from the inner city with one from the more 'plush' areas to see how far our judgements were based socially, politically and in terms of work functioning on our Christian beliefs and how far they simply reflected the class, social or work background or area from which we came.

On one weekend we brought together members of churches from Purley, a fairly comfortable middle-class area of Surrey, and Peckham, a decidedly inner-city, mainly working-class parish. It was the eve of a general election, and so we started the weekend by light-heartedly asking, 'How are those of you from Purley/Peckham going to vote?' Not surprisingly Purley was overwhelmingly Conservative and Peckham equally Labour. We then said with a slight degree of irony: 'Isn't this remarkable? Two groups of Christians – to one the Holy Spirit gives one kind of political guidance and only six miles away the Holy Spirit utters different guidance!' One of the members replied, 'Don't be silly. It's nothing to do with the Holy Spirit. It's to do with whether you live in Purley or Peckham.' 'All right,' we said, 'that is a good starting point. Why are our views as Christians determined not by the Gospel but by the conditioning of our background? Why are our political views not determined by the mind of Christ but by where we live and the position we hold in society?'

The experience of listening to the laity led to the asking of many questions: First, why do the churches concern themselves so much more with personal morality (usually matters of sexuality) than with the corporate issues which engage men and women in their working, civic and political life? Why also are we able to say much more clearly what is right and wrong in sexual issues than in issues of wealth and poverty, homelessness, oppression, force and violence? (Christ said little or nothing about sex but a great deal in parable and teaching about the latter. However, the church seems largely to have reversed the priorities of Christ.)

Secondly, since the most important part of a lay person's life is spent not in church but in the world, and it is there that most of his or her important decisions will have to be made if the command to extend the kingdom of God is to be obeyed, then why is so much time demanded of the laity for the propping up of largely uninfluential churches? Is

19

this because the whole organisation of a church is geared to what the clergy want and the reinforcement of their authority rather than to the true needs of the laity?

From the Southwark Ordination Course and other such systems of clergy training there were great hopes that this linking of clergy training with secular life and work would produce a non-stipendiary clergy who, by maintaining that link, would see their priesthood as within and through their work rather than through the local church. Unfortunately, in all but a few cases this has not been the case. The institutional church has seen them as weekend helpers of the clergy in rather the same way as the laity, and most have accepted the role of weekend priest, making a separation between their daily work and their priesthood. Many also who started as non-stipendiary have been lured into giving up their secular employment after a few years and have become just parish clergy like their fellow stipendiaries. Even worse, no sooner do they become stipendiary parish clergy than they too fall into seeing their task as maintaining the fabric of a diminishing church rather than as fellow-promoters with the laity of extending the kingdom of God in the world.

5

RETURN TO THE PARISH – CAMBERWELL

After seven years as director of lay training I felt that the time had come for someone else to take on this specialist work and for me to apply what I had learnt from the laity back in the parish. I feel strongly that specialist work in the church has to be tested out in the areas of everyday life, and for most of us clergy that has to mean in the parish. Moreover, specialist work needs the constant fertilising of new techniques and ideas, and so one person should not stay in it too long. To a certain type of person specialist posts can be a temptation – a way of escape from the realities of life into the realm of theorising. It can also be tempting to think of oneself as an 'expert', showing the poor inferior clergy how to do their work! To be a diocesan missioner, a director of post-ordination or lay training, a stewardship or education director can imply that you are the authority on mission, training, stewardship or education, and that can be very dangerous. It can easily lead to a belief in personal infallibility all too often seen in bishops and priests from the Pope downwards!

So back I went to the parish, a large inner-city parish, Camberwell. There I could begin to test out what I had learnt from my years in lay training – namely, to listen to lay people and to gear preaching, teaching, study and organisation to enabling the laity to fulfil their true potential, not in the church but in the world. Camberwell, like many other inner-city areas, consisted not of one community but of many. There were fine Georgian houses dating back to the days when Camberwell housed the wealthy merchants from

21

the City of London, now restored and lived in by people in executive positions who preferred to live near the city rather than to commute. But the vast majority of the population lived in high-rise flats, many of them 'grotty' and impersonal.

Just as there were two white groups, the wealthy and the poor, who had little contact with each other, so there were two black groups, of West Indian and Nigerian ethnic origin, who similarly had little in common. Many different life-styles were also to be found: professional people including doctors and psychiatrists employed at important hospitals in the area; one-parent families and many-parent families in community, and a considerable number of 'gay' relationships. The St Giles Centre, in the crypt of the church and occupying part of the building opposite, provided shelter and counselling help for alcoholics and drug addicts.

So amidst all this what was to be the task of the church if it was to contribute something to the world around it? Within the congregation there was the usual one per cent of all the groups I have mentioned. We drew together this one per cent into meetings where they could thresh out their differences and, if necessary, confront each other and vent their anger. In this way better understanding could be, and was, generated which then could permeate, through the members, to others in the area with whom they associated. In other words the task of the church in a pluralistic community must be to contribute towards better relationships between each section within that community. Lay training could aim at no better work than to help the better functioning of the often antagonistic groups within pluralistic inner-city areas.

The other main task was to realise that the mission of Christ to the poor, the prisoners, the oppressed, meant that, as far as possible, both clergy and laity must try to enter into these various groups within the area and to be a public voice for their needs to the local borough council, the social services and the local press. This required a church which was both supportive and non-judgemental but had no illusions or false sentimentality about the realities of an often grim and violent area.

6

PASTORAL CARE AND COUNSELLING

One of the most valued experiences of my life and ministry has been the connection over more than twenty years with the work of support groups and training in pastoral care and counselling. This experience arose from the realisation of the great gap between theory and fact regarding the church as the Christian community it is supposed to be. In the early 1970s Mervyn Stockwood, then Bishop of Southwark, became alarmed about the number of personal difficulties arising among the clergy, either through domestic problems and marriage breakdown or with forms of stress caused by a sense of isolation and lack of support. He decided to appoint someone to give special attention to this work as personal adviser and counsellor to those in need of help. Canon Derek Blows was appointed to be the first diocesan adviser on pastoral care and counselling. (He later became director of the Westminster Pastoral Foundation.)

Derek soon realised that many of the problems of the clergy arose from the lack of groups in which they could find support and opportunity to share personal and work problems. Despite the claims of the church to be a community, the structures actually make this very difficult. A community is based upon openness, sharing and equality of status but the structures of the church are hierarchical – from bishop to archdeacon, from archdeacon to rural dean, from rural dean to vicar, from vicar to laity, or in terms of administration from General Synod to diocesan synods to deanery synods to parochial church councils. (I speak of the structures of the Church of England but those of the Roman Catholic Church and the non-conformist churches are also in varying degrees based on authority from above, whether priestly or some form of lay eldership.) These structures may be necessary for administrative purposes but they offer little opportunity for genuine human sharing of problems in openness of trust and confidentiality. As Moltmann says, community must come from below rather than from above:

> If people in our society are again to be able to live more human lives, then we must build up communities from below and recognise that we can only develop our personalities in relationships and communities ... in communities we become rich: rich in friends, in neighbours and colleagues, brothers and sisters, on whom we can rely in emergencies. Together as a community we can help ourselves in most difficulties. Together, in solidarity, we are strong enough to shape our destiny.[1]

Acting then on the belief that the clergy and laity needed such grass-roots communities, Derek circulated all the clergy and professional lay workers in the diocese in an attempt to discover whether they shared his feelings. The response was considerable – more than two hundred wrote to say that support groups would be of great help. As a result, such groups were formed all over the Diocese of Southwark. These groups met weekly, with breaks for holidays, in private houses for one and a half hours. Numbers were restricted to twelve and there was no agenda save what each member wished to bring relating to work or personal problems. Each group had two co-leaders, usually one clergy and one lay person who was nearly always female – to balance the sexes until such time as clergy also were of both sexes. These co-leaders were trained in counselling, and their work was simply to be enablers for the most effective functioning of the group. I have been such a co-leader now for twenty years, first in Southwark and now in Chichester diocese, and I can truthfully say that nothing in the official structures of the church has been so valuable to me as those groups. Through them I and other members of the groups have learnt ways of distinguishing between our own personal anxieties and those of the people we meet and for whom we have pastoral care. We have also deepened our understanding of problems through sharing the resources of others who may have faced and sometimes resolved similar problems. Learning through observation and participation what happens within the many groups in which we are involved in life, we recognise many human needs – the need to listen to others with proper attention, the need to share emotions as well as thoughts (in the groups members have felt able at times to cry, to be angry, to express joy and sorrow in a way we rarely can elsewhere, even within our own circle of family and friends).

Inevitably, the experience of sharing problems has led to the need to learn how better to help ourselves and others in particular areas of difficulty. As a result, those responsible for pastoral care and counselling within the diocese have set up study days and sometimes residential weekends to consider together such matters as: bereavement counselling; dealing with conflict and resolution of conflict; recognition of stress and coping with it; the experience of living alone; terminal illness and long-term support; worship and pastoral care; growing old and retirement.

The response to these study days and workshops has indicated how little attention has been paid by the church to the deeper needs of human nature and how often the church, which has claimed to be a loving community, not only shows ignorance but even insensitivity and judgementalism towards those in most need. But we cannot be a loving community unless we are prepared to experience and learn what community means and what in ourselves and our structures of working impedes that learning.

Kenneth Leech is right to be suspicious of counselling as simply an individual problem-solving exercise:

> One of the most damaging features of church life has been the reduction of pastoral ministry to a counselling model. The counsellor who is concerned with problem solving and derives his or her skills mainly from clinical and psychotherapeutic sources comes to be a model of Christian pastoral care. But this represents a grave

25

distortion of what pastoral care is about. To reduce pastoral ministry to counselling is a distortion which fits very comfortably within the individualist framework of thought but takes no account of the social theology of the Scriptures where emphasis is on the people of God, the Kingdom, the Body of Christ, the new creation. Pastoral care in the Christian tradition is a ministry of the whole community.[2]

But Kenneth Leech fails to emphasise that it is precisely because the church has failed to exercise a ministry of the whole community that an individualistic kind of social service and clinical ministry has taken the place of what should have been the functions of the ordinary cleric and lay person.

If all the local church can do is to cope with those who conform to and are happy with the conventional model of middle-class society, and is at a loss as to how to deal with those who want real sharing, real freedom to be themselves in expression of feelings however disturbing, then obviously the person in need of such an outlet will have to seek some kind of professional individual help. The groups I have been describing are seeking to exercise pastoral care within a small community which is a microcosm of the whole church as it is meant to be. That is their value. I shall have more to say about this in Part 3 when I consider, in the light of my experience, the future shape of the church if it is to fulfil its task as the agent of the forthcoming kingdom of God.

1 Jurgen Moltmann, *Creating a Just Future* (SCM Press 1989), p. 9.
2 Kenneth Leech, *Care and Conflict* (Darton, Longman and Todd 1990), p. 111.

7

A VILLAGE PARISH –
WOLDINGHAM

In 1976 I moved to an area very different from Camberwell – the commuter village, set in lovely North Downs Surrey countryside, of Woldingham. It was to be my last parish before retirement, the only time in my ministry when I was to be mainly concerned not with the problems of the poor but rather the stresses and difficulties of the rich! Woldingham was socially and geographically cut off from the world around it and, on the whole, rejoiced in its isolation. Many of the people living there held important and successful positions in industry, commerce or the professions; their work lay outside the village as did their main responsibilities and stresses. They came back to Woldingham at weekends to enjoy the relaxation of their large houses and gardens and they were fierce in their resistance to anything that might encroach upon the amenities of the neighbourhood and their properties. Within the village there was a very real sense of community but it was a strongly self-defensive community.

So how did the text and context relate in such a society? First, it was clear that the real context of their lives lay outside Woldingham. It was in that world of city, executive leadership, jet-setting round the world for productive enterprise, that decisions of ethical and moral responsibility had to be made – decisions which would affect not only themselves but many others, either as employees, clients or colleagues, and not forgetting the consumer. It was in that world that stresses and anxieties arose from the instability of economic life which could not easily be shared either

27

with colleagues in the same business or profession or with spouses and families. If the church then was to be of any reality to these people, it would not be through organising their social lives within the village – they were quite capable as a village community of organising such social life as they wanted – but rather through enabling them to think through and share the problems they encountered as Christians trying to relate their beliefs and faith to the world of power and accountability in which they moved from Monday to Friday.

It came to me, and nothing has ever come more directly as guidance of the Holy Spirit, that what they needed was regular opportunity to share with their peers the whole area of working life. So was born the Woldingham Business and Professional Group which has now been meeting regularly for over ten years. The group meets in a private house (members act as host in turn) on a Sunday morning once a month, strictly from 11.30 a.m. to 1 p.m. (Sunday morning proved to be the best time to meet since drinks before lunch on a Sunday was a common feature of Woldingham life and it is always best to fit in with the 'mores' of a place.) The issues discussed at meetings are raised by the members themselves and have included 'Redundancy', 'Commercial and Advertising Integrity', 'Multinational Corporations', 'Differing Standards in International Business Life', 'Trust', 'Responsibilities of Personal Wealth', 'Medical Ethics', 'Problems of Teaching', 'Trades Unionism and Management', 'Retirement', and many others. My task as parish priest was mainly to listen, understand and learn, and from time to time be a kind of theological resource person putting in questions from an ethical or theological stance. I was asked recently to celebrate their first ten years by producing a paper highlighting some present ethical concerns. I posed the following questions: Is the consumerist society a good society contributing to the needs and happiness of human beings? Do we have a divided nation in which it is taken for granted that one life-style is and ought to be appropriate for the rich and one for the poor? Is it a true assumption (based upon Margaret Thatcher's address to the Church of Scotland) that wealth carries a sense of greater responsibility for the poor? Is a growth economy compatible with care for the environment? These questions have since posed many heart-searching sessions for the group, because they were their problems.

I am glad that my last experience of parochial ministry before retirement was in a very different social area from the previous one. Had I not had that experience I might never have realised so forcibly that there is a ministry to the rich as well as to the poor, and it is a ministry which must be exercised without either collusion or evasion. There are areas which the church must challenge (and also challenge within itself), but the challenge must be made with under-standing of the pressures. No priest must pontificate in any area of life in which he has not had experience unless he is prepared to listen and learn from those who are involved. So often the clergy have earned, and rightly earned, con-tempt for preaching and writing in the parish magazine or through the media in a way which shows no real understand-ing of business and economic life, or else for currying favour with the rich. In the words of St James,

> Suppose you pay special attention to the well-dressed man and say to him, 'Please take this seat,' while to the poor man you say, 'You can stand; or you may sit here on the floor by my footstool,' do you not see that you are inconsistent and judge by false standards? (James 2:3–4)

29

8

RETIREMENT

While living in West Sussex in retirement it has become all too obvious to me how little attention is paid to the training which relates text to the context of society. Most of the churches in the area in which I live are still run on the basis that apart from the regular worship the only activities organised will be for the benefit of the congregation; very little reference is made to the far greater number of people who rarely or never form part of that congregation. Most social activity is separatist – groups for women, for youth, for children (rarely for men) – and all mainly for the benefit of those within the church. Even when local churches hold study groups or campaigns for evangelism there seems little evidence that these have any marked effect. The laity do not see their work as mainly in the society around them, and the clergy's ministry and visiting are concentrated mainly on the one per cent within the church rather than the ninety-nine per cent outside.

It seems that the parable of the lost sheep has been reversed – the ninety-nine are ignored while excessive attention is given to the whims and often very inflexible views of the one per cent within the fold. What are we doing when we pray, 'Thy kingdom come'? Unless more of our training of both clergy and laity is geared to the permeation of the work, economics, social and political life of the secular world, we might as well stop praying that prayer, for no kingdom will ever come!

I have found that 'retirement' for a priest is seldom really retirement but rather a choice of which ministry one chooses to continue. Apart from 'helping out' on most Sundays – in times of sickness, holidays, sabbaticals and *interregna* as preacher or celebrant in many different kinds of parishes – I also assist with the teaching of ethics at Chichester Theological College and take a considerable part in the educational and group work of the Council for Pastoral Care in the diocese. The work I have been doing in retirement has added to my understanding of ministry in two ways:

First, I have learnt valuable lessons in humility – as merely a 'visiting locum' I have to accept what I am given whether I like it or not. Secondly, teaching ethics to future ministers has not only enabled me to keep in touch with the thinking of the younger generation and with the women being trained as deacons but has also kept my own thinking up to date.

Part Two

THE PRESENT SITUATION

9

REALITY IN BELIEF: DENIAL OR ESCAPE

Viewed from the background I have described, it seems to me that the present situation of the church can be summed up as denial or escape from reality in most areas of life.

I take as my definition of realism 'the tendency to look at, accept or represent things as they really are'. This is the basis also on which Dr William Glasser has founded 'reality therapy', a treatment now used in the field of psychiatry. Dr Glasser, in describing reality therapy, says:

> In their unsuccessful efforts to fulfil their needs all patients have a common characteristic: they all deny the reality of the world around them. Therapy will be successful when they are able to give up denying the world and recognise that reality not only exists but that they must fulfil their needs within its framework.[1]

What is true of psychiatric experience is also true of society as a whole and of the church itself. Because of a widely held but false view of the realities of human existence, God is looked upon as a reassuring background to life and, to a large extent, the church has encouraged that illusion in both its preaching and its ways of organisation. This false view of the realities of life is based upon the idea fostered by secular society that human beings have a natural right to happiness. This is nowhere justified in the Bible or in human experience, but it is very persistent and is even enshrined in the American Constitution:

35

> We hold these truths to be self-evident: that all men are created equal, that they are endowed by their Creator with certain inalienable rights, that among these are life, liberty and the pursuit of happiness.

But the reality is that in the world of human beings there is no natural right to happiness given to human beings by God, nor indeed are we created equal – equal maybe in the sight of God, but certainly not equal in human health, wealth or advantages of life. And the Book of Job should have dispelled for all time the idea that human virtue and human happiness necessarily go together. Yet these illusions persist. Many Christians have to admit that, when it comes to be tested by life, 'their faith has become unreal, and that this unreality stems precisely from their efforts to be honest with their actual experience, with the echo of the contemporary world and its questions sounding within themselves'.[2]

We are still expected to be able to explain how we can believe in a loving God in the face of great natural disasters, like the floods in Bangladesh, starvation in Ethiopia, earthquakes and the fate of the Kurds, whereas no explanation is necessary. Such disasters in reality are either the result of human abuse of the environment (the cutting down of trees in Nepal or Brazil), of the corruption of governments which prefer to waste money on civil wars rather than feed their people, or of the geological formation of the world which is simply an amoral fact.

Moreover, great pressure is put upon clergy to explain individual suffering – 'Why should this happen to *me*?' – and much bitterness and alienation from the church has arisen because the answer has not been convincing. But why should it be? There is no answer, no more than there would be if in the middle of joy and happiness I ask the question, 'Why should this happen to *me*?' – which, of course, I never do. Such is the inborn nature of human egocentricity.

Sadly, many of the present apparently 'successful' religious groups are those which have succumbed to the temptation to provide God as a reassuring background to life. Faced with the realities of life these groups avoid them and become emotional ghettos of fundamentalism encapsulated from the world and its realities. They provide a privatised religion of individual feelings of comfort and pseudo-security – a sense of being 'saved' or 'born again', of being received into a comfortable charismatic club of outward cheerfulness and closed community far removed from the world's struggles.

Some people seem to rejoice that the fundamentalist and charismatic churches are full of young people, that these churches are drawing large congregations. I certainly can admire the enthusiasm, the sense of community, the use of the body in worship which usually exists in such churches, but there my admiration stops. Anyone who can seriously entertain a concept of the truth of the Bible which relies upon the factual accuracy of every statement within it and who refuses to face the critical questions with which biblical research and scholarship confront us is not only confusing faith with naïve credulity but has no understanding of the reality of truth.

Truth as understood by the biblical writers had no such narrow technical definitions, and the writers of the Pentateuch would have seriously doubted the sanity of anyone wanting to pin them down to a seven-day Creation, the Garden of Eden as a geographical situation, Noah's Ark as an actually constructed boat or Balaam's speaking donkey as a fact of experience. To treat the poetic truth of the Bible as if it must be subjected to the narrow analysis of the pseudo-scientific, secularised society is to misunderstand the meaning of reality. Reality does not lie in technical facts; this is the mistake made by fundamentalists. Reality lies in the meaning behind the facts.

D. H. Lawrence put this well when he said: 'If you try to nail everything down it either kills the reality or the reality gets up and walks away with the nails.' Poets and mystics are often better at discovering the true reality of religion than so-called religious people!

Moreover, I cannot believe that a religion which substitutes emotional enthusiasm, naïve dogmatism and much ingrown community life for genuine searching for truth, hard questioning and true faith – which grows and matures through doubt and through wrestling with the issues of the world around it – will have much staying power. In much populist religion of today there appears to be a spirit of 'the more we are together the merrier we shall be', but, as Bonhoeffer has rightly said, 'religion is not a reassuring background music to life.'[3] Kenneth Leech sums up the dangers of such populism when he says:

> The fate of such believers can be really terrible, for the slightest doubt can lead to total collapse and loss of faith. For they have become like an iron bridge with no 'give' in it, and from apparently believing everything without question, they cease to believe anything.[4]

The other question I would raise on much fundamentalist evangelical religion today is: why is it that so much of it, especially in the United States and frequently even here, goes along with very right-wing politics? The Moral Majority of America was notorious for its support of Reagan's policies against the left-wing governments in Latin America and it even justified nuclear war, seeming to see in it the Armageddon of the Bible. Perhaps Don Cupitt has the answer to this question:

> ... the more anti-intellectual the faith, the more vulnerable it is to politicisation. The church's defences against modern thought are at the same time gateways for the entrance of modern politics. Knowing this, politicians invariably urge a simple populist faith upon the church. It will make her easier for them to control. And a populist Christianity that in effect serves the interests of the political right becomes thereby just as much secularised as a church that has been taken over by the political left.[5]

I find it very difficult to understand why people who make such great claims to be 'saved', to 'know Jesus' and to base their entire thinking and life on what is written in the Scriptures should so neglect the teaching of the prophets and Jesus' own teaching on the kingdom of God as to be able to accept, without question, the dominance given these days to the market economy and a political philosophy that unquestionably has a bias towards the rich rather than the poor. Jim Wallis, speaking as an American evangelical, criticises this attitude:

> Throughout evangelical training and experience there is no clear proclamation of the Kingdom of God. By neglecting the Kingdom of God in our preaching, we have lost the integrating and central core of the Gospel. The disastrous result is 'saved' individuals who comfortably fit into the old order, while the new order goes unannounced. The social meaning of conversion is lost and a privatised gospel supports the *status quo*.[6]

So, while the fundamentalist and charismatic sects encourage escape from reality, among the mainstream churches there is often a denial of reality: the Anglican Church, for example, often tries to enforce a theology or ethic which does not meet the actual situation. And in its training of clergy and laity the church escapes from confrontation and struggle with the real forces of the world in order to retreat into a small area of cosy existence which makes little impact on the world around it.

We might paraphrase the words by Dr Glasser, quoted at the beginning of this chapter, by saying that if as Christians we wish to be of real value to the world around us we must also 'recognise that reality not only exists but that we must fulfil our needs within its framework'.

The failure of the church to recognise reality shows itself in every sphere. Regarding its dealing with issues of sexuality Kenneth Leech says:

> I am increasingly troubled by the deep fear of human passion and sexuality which seems so deeply rooted in the Christian Church. If sexuality and sexual energy is the raw material of sanctity, why is it that the church seems to be the one place where serious debate on these issues is not possible? So much Christian discourse on sexuality is based in illusion.[7]

The nature of this illusion I will deal with later.

In matters of theological thinking the same gap exists between what is theological orthodoxy and what is actually thought. Don Cupitt writes:

An important but neglected feature of the spiritual disorder of the times is that today there is sharp conflict between individual and group belief. For at least a century there have been people who think that the machinery by which groups of every sort generate and maintain their ideologies and their power is now sufficiently well-understood and discredited for it to be impossible any more for a reflective person to submit to any authority and accept its creed . . . One should live in the hills and walk in the free air, an alien and a wanderer suspicious of all creeds and organisations and owing no allegiance to any of them . . . The churches seem to be planning to become slowly more rigid as they shrink . . . they have largely disinvested in critical theology and are instead taking up various forms of theological populism.[8]

Kenneth Leech says very much the same:

Hence the tragic, but all too common, phenomenon of the Christian believer, whether Catholic or evangelical variety, who protects himself or herself from any real critique or threat by an acquired jargon. Certainties and pious clichés are repeated parrot-fashion, real dialogue becomes impossible, and conflict and questioning are systematically repressed.[9]

There is also, among traditionalist and radical thinkers a failure to make any impact on the widespread indifference to religion which is the average attitude today. Even for many Christians God does not offer any satisfactory explanation of the problems and tragedies of human life. The non-relevance of God is accepted, for all practical and living purposes, as a normal state of affairs. I shall be looking at this further in chapter 14.

It has to be admitted that this general sense of irrelevance affects not only established forms of religious and credal beliefs, but almost all ideologies which claim to have answers to questions of philosophy or meaning in life. The humanistic liberalism of the last century is wearing very thin, now that the present confusion and state of the world gives little ground for faith in human omnipotence. Technological progress has certainly not resulted in progress in man's humanity to man; in fact it has increased rather than diminished the capacity of human beings to destroy themselves through either nuclear warfare or environmental damage. It is becoming increasingly clear that cleverness without wisdom may lead as much to our destruction as any other aspect of human nature. In the words of E. F. Schumacher:

> Man closed the gates of heaven against himself and tried, with immense energy and ingenuity, to confine himself to the earth. He is now discovering that the earth is but a transitory state, so that a refusal to reach for heaven means an involuntary descent into hell.[10]

Even within the minority who belong to churches and claim religious belief it is often difficult to know what is meant by religious belief. Each week most church congregations say together the Creed, but many church members have grave doubts about the virgin birth, would be hard put to it to say what they mean by the Trinity of God the Father, God the Son and God the Holy Spirit, or explain the relationship between the humanity and divinity of Christ. Most would be more than sceptical about a 'second coming' and, as one finds at times of bereavement, belief in life after death is often more a pious hope than a firm belief. It is always interesting to me that many who claim to be traditionalists, and who are shocked and angered by the radicalism of the Bishop of Durham, when tackled about their own beliefs in the resurrection of Christ, will be quite happy with teaching that emphasises the coming alive of Christ to the consciousness of the disciples and consequent coming alive of their life and faith rather than emphasising the empty tomb. (And this is exactly what Bishop Jenkins is saying and what I have myself preached for years without 'shocking' anyone!) There is something naturally simplistic in most people that makes them respond to what seems reasonable to them and, as a result, ethics has far more place than doctrine in their thinking.

I am not saying that this is desirable. In many ways it is not, because it leads to lazy thinking about religion which would not be accepted in any other field of thought, but as a fact of life it has to be faced. Ask many churchgoers what Christianity is and you will often receive little more than phrases about morality: 'being good and kind to each other', 'following the example of Jesus', 'going to church regularly', 'not committing any flagrant sins' (usually sexual!), 'doing good works and helping people'.

One of the most pathetic facts in the situation of the church today is the sheer ignorance of most churchgoers about their religion. In an age of much sceptical and intelligent questioning all that most Christians can do is either to repeat dogmatic evangelical phrases – like 'being born again', 'baptised by the Spirit', 'knowing Jesus', 'being saved' – which mean little or nothing to the outsider – or to fall back on a vague semi-humanistic ethic which has little to do with religious truth. Knowledge of the searchings of theology is restricted to a small group of academics who seem unable to communicate that knowledge in a language that can be widely understood. The parish clergyman, to whom that communication is entrusted, often seems to forget in his preaching and teaching all he learned in college and falls back on a vague moralism with little bite or relevance.

1 William Glasser, *Reality Therapy*, Harper and Row 1965.
2 Claude Geffre in an article in *Concilium*, 165, p. 61.
3 Dietrich Bonhoeffer, *Ethics* (Fontana 1964), p. 230.
4 Kenneth Leech, *True God* (Sheldon Press 1985), p. 25.
5 Don Cupitt, *Radicals and the Future of the Church* (SCM Press 1989), p. 91.
6 Jim Wallis, *Call to Conversion*, quoted in K. Leech, *Spirituality and Pastoral Care* (Sheldon Press 1986), p. 34.
7 Kenneth Leech, *Care and Conflict* (Darton, Longman and Todd 1990), p. 85.
8 Cupitt, op. cit., p. 7.
9 Leech, *True God*, p. 25.
10 E. F. Schumacher, *A Guide for the Perplexed* (Jonathan Cape 1977), p. 153.

10

SEXUALITY AND REALITY

REALISM OR FANTASY

In no area of life has the church been so incapable of realistic and creative thinking and action as in the realm of sexuality. This shows itself in many ways. While upholding the doctrine of the permanence and indissolubility of marriage the church has largely failed to take into account the stresses of increasing longevity of life, changed attitudes regarding male/female partnership and male/female roles, and many other factors which contribute to a serial rather than a permanent view of married life.

Nor has the church found a constructive way of dealing with marriage failure. In the Church of England, after nearly ten years of argument in General Synod, we have rejected all possible ways forward and arrived at the ridiculous situation where each parish priest makes his own decision as to whether or not to remarry a divorced person. So if you live in one parish you will be accepted, in another refused. Or else we go through the polite farce of what is called 'blessing' of a civil marriage, where we say: 'We cannot technically marry you but we will give you what looks to the outside world exactly like a wedding, often even to the bridal white, the hymns, the bells and all the trimmings.' In other words we pretend: we are saying that theologically divorced people are committing adultery in remarrying, while we treat them socially and religiously as a truly married couple, which in fact by law they are.

We are involved in the same strange contradictions with regard to birth control – an incapacity to face reality. The Pope goes to countries where there is vast over-population, which contributes to extreme poverty, and talks there about the immorality of birth control. The Church of England believes officially that sexual relationship is for procreation but countenances non-procreational sex so long as it is within the confines of official marriage, without seeing the illogicality in viewing the same non-procreational act as an expression of love in one situation but as wicked and immoral in another.

In dealing with homosexuals the church has never been able to face reality. Despite the factual reality that a homosexual is simply someone who, for some reason, which no one quite understands, is not sexually attracted to the opposite sex, the church persists in regarding him or her as a deliberately perverse person who is just choosing, out of wickedness, to act differently from normal. Or alternatively he or she is regarded as sick or disabled, but despite that is rarely given the compassion and understanding that we usually give to disabled or sick people. One would think that if society and the church really believe that human happiness is through marriage and family, there would be overwhelming sympathy for those who, through no fault of their own but simply through parental mis-relationship or hormone accident, are deprived of both. If it were so, one would expect there to be a discriminating pity and welcome for such lonely people, but in fact there are few signs of that in either church or society. A few churchmen even wish to deprive homosexual clergy of the mitigation of their loneliness by sharing the vicarage with another person. When I revealed that I belonged to this sexual minority I was barred altogether from officiating in a church where I had previously often preached. Far from being shown warmth and love as towards someone damaged, I was excluded like a leper because, as the vicar put it, 'the church must be kept pure'! I had not changed in any way from the person accepted and even praised for his preaching, save that I had revealed a truth about my personality.

The other unreality expected of the homosexual is that the complete celibacy expected will be easy to bear. No one ever explains why it should be assumed that the sexual urge is any less powerful for the homosexual than it is for the average heterosexual.

Sherwin Bailey, writing of earlier centuries, says:

44

The general impression left by the churches' teaching upon simple and unlearned people can only have been that the physical relationship of the sexes was regarded by religion as unworthy if not shameless and obscene. The effect of such teaching must necessarily have been grave; it caused a distortion of principles and values which have left an indelible mark on Christian sexual thought, and we can only guess at the psychological disturbance and conflicts which it has produced in the lives of individuals.[1]

The idea that sexuality is somehow unclean has dominated religious thinking and attitudes for many generations. William Countryman, in a very comprehensive and detailed account of the origins of the church's sexual ethics, shows that they were based, on the one hand, on ideas of ritual purity and, on the other, on a property ethic rooted in male domination and inheritance.[2]

There are many examples of the incapacity to unite sexuality and spirituality and of the idea that somehow sexuality is unclean:

1. In the Old Testament there were many occasions when the seeking of God's will necessitated abstention from intercourse between men and their wives.

2. The early Christian Fathers found it very difficult to accept sexuality as a natural and joyful part of human living. Clement of Alexandria claimed that 'the best Christians are those that are married but have no sexual relationship with their wives'! Tertullian regarded marriage as a necessity but one to be deprecated. Augustine developed this into a theology in which sexuality was the result of the Fall: enjoyment of the flesh constituted a barrier to the enjoyment of God (one can trace the bitter struggle Augustine had with his own sexual passions here). Marriage had to be allowed and coitus practised, but it must not be enjoyed. Medieval canonists debated whether married couples should receive Holy Communion if they had made love the previous night. St Bernadine of Siena held that it was mortal sin not to abstain from sexual intercourse before communion. Somehow sexuality was regarded as the carnal nature which could

45

not be joined with the spiritual nature. Sexual activity could be justified only on a biological basis and not on a personal basis, despite its closest association with the highest of Christian ideals, namely love.

A study of recent papal encyclicals shows how little ideas have changed since Tertullian wrote 'On Purity' and Augustine wrote 'On Virginity'.

3. The Roman Catholic Church taught for centuries that during certain seasons of the year, notably Lent, sexual intercourse should be abstained from, even in marriage.

4. Until fairly recently the service of the Churching of Women was not only regarded as an act of thanksgiving for the birth of a child but also as a kind of purification of the woman, after the old style of Jewish law. Indeed in my Devonian village when I was a child it was still regarded as not respectable for a woman who had given birth to go out and mix with people until she had been churched.

5. St Paul quite clearly asserted that continence is best and that marriage and sexual relationship is second-best: 'Now concerning the things whereof ye wrote unto me: it is good for a man not to touch a woman. Nevertheless, to avoid fornication, let every man have his own wife, and let every woman have her own husband.' (1 Corinthians 7:1–2 AV)

It is often said that Paul only said that because of his belief in the imminence of the Second Coming. If that were so, it is strange that the Church of England marriage service, as drawn up in the 1662 Prayer Book and generally used until recently, echoed the same words even though there was by then no expectation of an imminent Second Coming: 'Secondly, marriage was ordained as a remedy against sin and to avoid fornication that such persons as have not the gift of continency might marry and keep themselves undefiled members of Christ's body.' Note the subtle implication that marriage is a slightly second-rate state for 'such as have not the gift of continency'. Why 'the gift'? It would be a sad state for the world if everyone had the gift of continency! There seems always to have been in the church this idea that the virgin or celibate is in some sense a higher mortal. Does this account for the emphases laid upon the Virgin Birth of Christ, the Immaculate Conception of the Virgin

Mary, the necessity that Christ should never appear to have had any sexual relationship, the stress on celibacy for Roman Catholic priests? Does it also account for the undue prominence that sexual sin has had in the judgements of the church through the ages as compared with other personal 'deadly sins' and corporate sin? We hear of priests being disciplined for sexual sins but we rarely hear of a priest being disciplined for pride, envy, covetousness, sloth, gluttony or anger – the other listed deadly sins. It seems that the church cannot rejoice in the joys of sexuality but must always have a sort of government-health-warning attitude towards it!

BACKGROUND TO THE CHURCH'S ATTITUDE TO SEXUALITY

There are various reasons for this attitude, most of them reflecting the sociological practices of the Jewish peoples and their need for defences against pagan religions rather than any specific Christian emphasis. In fact Jesus says practically nothing about sexuality except in relation to questions asked of him regarding the legality of divorce and in order to emphasise his general teaching that it is the motivation behind actions which is important. For example, the condemnation of homosexual practice as one of the worst sexual sins finds no echo in Jesus; he never once mentions the subject in any of the gospels.

The various reasons behind the church's uncreative attitude to sexuality are:

1. The Old Testament reflected the states of Israel and Judah, both male-dominated societies and two small countries needing population growth to increase their strength. The safeguarding of procreation was important. It was thought then that life was formed by the male's production of life-giving seed not, as we now know, by the production of the human ovum by the female in conjunction with the male seed. Polygamy was accepted as part of a culture in which the tribal extended family was the basic social unit. Men were not subject to strict sexual mores, but women

were – they were the property of their husbands. It was necessary therefore to protect women against impurity and men against impotence, hence the laws against masturbation and homosexuality or any other kind of sexuality which did not involve procreation.

2. Jewish sexual practices were also connected with the Canaanite Baal worship that surrounded the Jewish states. In order to protect the worship of Yahweh there had to be strict rules against any forms of genital practice which might seem to resemble what went on in idolatrous temples. Nevertheless, within the Old Testament we do, on the whole, find a positive view of sexuality. In creation the flesh is the vehicle of the spirit: man is made in the image of God; woman is made from the flesh of man. The whole emphasis is on the unity of the whole person, indeed the word 'flesh' in the Old Testament means the entire human being. Sexual union is not mere animal gratification but a constant movement towards communion in love, which is the goal of life. In the Old Testament sexuality comes through as a gift; it is to be celebrated and enjoyed. Nowhere is the joy of sexuality more celebrated, in heterosexual terms, than in the Song of Solomon and, in homosexual terms, in the story of David and Jonathan. In the former the bridegroom addressing his bride dwells on her flesh in all its loveliness and desirability; in the latter David and Jonathan physically and lovingly embrace and their love is described as 'passing the love of women'.

3. In the New Testament a sense of the dividedness of flesh and spirit begins in the thinking of St Paul. He taught that flesh and spirit were at war with each other, but by 'the flesh' he meant natural man as distinct from spiritual man. Owing, however, to the influence of Greek thought – for Paul was a Greek scholar – 'the flesh' came more and more to mean the human body and its desires, of which sex was one of the strongest. The general idea in much Greek philosophy was that man is a dualism of a soul fettered to a body, brought down by a body, and often at war with the body. It is easy to see how this thinking gradually led to the Manichaean heresy

48

that the flesh is evil. Even though this thinking was condemned, nevertheless it lingered on in the writings of the
Fathers, who could not bring themselves to think of sexual
activity as something to be enjoyed.

Added to this thinking was the fact that Christians in such
centres as Rome and Corinth were surrounded by one of
the most debauched societies in history, in which every kind
of sexual permissiveness was tolerated and practised, and
the lead in this given by the emperors. It was also an age
when both boy and girl prostitution were part of pagan
religious practices, so it was not surprising that Paul and the
early Christian fathers were suspicious of sexuality.

Although declared a heresy Manichaeism has had a profound influence through the generations on Christian and
non-Christian attitudes to sexuality. It led, on the one hand,
to puritanism – the flesh being evil must be strictly con-
trolled – or, on the other hand, to pornography – the flesh
being evil can be degraded. By a paradox puritanism and
pornography have the same parentage!

The elevation of marriage by Protestants and celibacy by
Catholics is another result of this polarisation of flesh and
spirit. Either sex is so dangerous it must be forsworn or it
must be channelled harmlessly into marriage.

As a result of these factors sexual activity has been justified
by the church for centuries on a biological rather than a
personal basis. This has meant that for millions of people
for whom marriage is denied – through their own sexual
orientation or for other reasons which make marriage
impossible – sexual activity is totally prohibited if they wish
to follow church teachings. What is called redemption of
sexuality means for them renunciation of their sexuality and
a compulsory celibacy – which not only degrades celibacy
but is probably neither desired nor fitting. However, things
are beginning to change to a moral assessment based on
the personal rather than the biological. Jack Dominion, a
Roman Catholic doctor, is one who has heralded this
change:

We are witnessing the end of the era which has linked

sexual pleasure predominantly with procreation . . . the shift from biology and physiology to person and love is a good beginning for the mammoth task ahead and one which is in keeping with the theology of Vatican II.[3]

It does not yet, however, seem to have permeated into the thinking on sexuality of either the Pope or the Vatican, nor into the evangelical or Anglo-Catholic areas of the Church of England.

MISCONCEPTIONS ABOUT HOMOSEXUALITY

The unreality of both the church's and society's attitudes becomes even more apparent when dealing with homosexuality. There is an emotional and traditional attitude, within both secular and religious circles, which for some reason views homosexuality amongst men with an abhorrence which arouses immediate feelings of attack and condemnation. Also, despite the fact that the subject has now been debated and exhaustively treated both medically and psychologically for many years, there is still an ignorance which one can sometimes only think is deliberately perpetuated. It shows itself in many different ways:

1. It is commonly assumed that homosexual men are also pederasts. I have more than once heard fear expressed that choir boys may be under threat from a bachelor priest but have never heard any fears that choir girls may be under threat from a heterosexual priest! There are human beings both male and female who have an attraction towards boys and girls under the age of puberty, but only a very small proportion of homosexuals have this kind of attraction and recent reports of child abuse show that far more small girls are in danger of sexual abuse than small boys. Nevertheless, the fiction persists and the law is often far more condemnatory towards offences against boys than against girls.

2. It is often feared that homosexuals will 'convert' heterosexuals; recent statements on sex education in schools, such

as clause 28, have had this suspicion in mind. Not long ago I heard on an 'Any Questions' programme a member of the panel objecting to an application for a Gay Club in her town on the grounds that some young men who would otherwise have been heterosexual might be 'tipped over' (her words) into homosexuality. There are some people, it is true, who are bisexual, and there are some who, in unusual forced circumstances of all-male society such as prisons or the forces, may practise homosexual intercourse but who, when released, will immediately revert to their norm, but it is unlikely that the true heterosexual will ever make a deliberate choice to be homosexual. In fact, it would be very strange if anyone should choose to become homosexual in our society, since it is obviously far easier to be with the majority rather than the minority in sexual orientation.

3. In the recent epidemic of AIDS, despite the overwhelming evidence that in most parts of the world it is predominantly a heterosexual disease and only in some areas, notably the USA, did it start from homosexual relationships, there are still many people who assume that it is the 'gay disease'. Many people are reluctant to admit that they may be HIV positive because it will then be assumed that they are 'gay'. Some ignorant comments about AIDS and homosexuality remind me of the words of a Lutheran theologian of the seventeenth century, Benedict Carpzov, who said the results of homosexual practice were 'earthquakes, famine, pestilence, Saracens, floods and very fat, voracious field mice' – a very interesting combination for which it would be fascinating to trace the connection!

4. Finally, the unreality persists in the different legal attitudes towards male and female homosexuality, commonly called lesbianism. Adult male homosexuality was until 1967 a criminal offence, and still is for those under 21. Never has it been so amongst women; how often does one hear of a lesbian arrested for offences against girls as compared with men arraigned for offences against teenagers?

The attitudes of society have to be noted, because it is quite obvious that, although the church claims support from

Scripture for its very strong and persistent attacks on homosexuals, there are far less references to this particular so-
called sin (none at all by Christ in the gospels) than there
are to many other forms of sin, and one can only conclude
that here as in many other ways the church is far more
influenced by the attitudes of society than by its own Christian affirmations.

Unfortunately, however, the so-called 'gay' world has
reacted with equal unreality to the position of the homosexual. It is understandable, in view of the very negative
attitudes of society, that homosexuals should have wanted a
more affirmative term, and so the term 'gay' has been
adopted. This makes the former use of that word now almost
impossible, but the image of the word 'gay' is as unreal as
the derisory word 'queer'. We have to use the word 'gay'
because of its universal adoption, but it conveys an image.
Homosexuals are no more or less gay than other people.
Some are, but many are far from being gay; they are often
depressed and guilt-ridden individuals, largely because of
society. 'Gay is good', one of the slogans frequently used,
may sound affirmative but it is not true. Being 'gay' is not
necessarily good, neither is being 'straight'. Many gay people
in our society would prefer not to be so, in fact probably
most, if they are honest, since being 'gay' presents more
difficulties than solutions and if relationship of a durable
nature is difficult in heterosexual society, it is often even
more difficult in homosexual society.

Moreover, the so-called 'gay' world is often no more
understanding and compassionate than the 'straight' world.
'Gay' clubs and pubs are not places where real friendship
and love may be found but rather 'pick-up' contact points
for one-night stands: if the face or the age does not fit, the
person will be ignored and so will experience an even
greater sense of loneliness and exclusion than he or she
would in a more general place of relaxation. As a result, the
same kind of negative unreality is found in the very world
that is loud in its protest against the attitudes of heterosexual
society – the unreality of assessment not by character or
personality but by genital activity. It is strangely ironic that
society, church and the 'gay' world itself are all obsessed

with the purely physical; what is done in bed becomes far more important, in terms of disapproval or approval, than creative human relationship.

1 Sherwin Bailey, *Homosexuality and the Western Tradition*, Longmans 1955.
2 William Countryman, *Dirt, Greed and Sex*, SCM Press 1988.
3 Jack Dominian, *Proposals for a New Sexual Ethic* (Darton, Longman and Todd 1977), pp. 23, 25.

11

COMMUNITY AND REALITY

As I indicated in chapter 6, good pastoral care depends on the church being a community. If we are to create the kind of community described there by Moltmann – namely, one which is built up from below – the whole structures of the churches, and particularly of the Church of England, must change. For at present the church seems to be modelling itself on recent efforts by the government to destroy local responsibility and to substitute it with centralisation.

In fact, there are several aspects of modern society as well as of the church which present obstacles to community. Perhaps the greatest is the overall trend away from small communities to the large centralised conurbation where 'small is beautiful' no longer holds. During the years of Thatcherite government the virtues of individualism and self-interest and independence have been officially proclaimed. Margaret Thatcher is reported to have said, 'There is no such thing as society'; whether or not that is true, the result has been a society in which each person is concerned with his or her own desires and goals and few care a great deal about others. In the struggle of competition, all against all, the upwardly mobile reach the top and, to quote Moltmann again:

> . . . since there is never enough for everyone more and more people are forced to the margin or oppressed. The ideology of 'there is not enough for everyone' makes people lonely, isolates them, deprives them of their relations with others and leads them to social death.[1]

This is noticeable in many ways in ordinary life, all adding up to loss of community in both town and country.

In Camberwell I used to see the old Peabody buildings with the common courtyard which everyone passed through, and around which most of the family – aunts and uncles, grandparents as well as parents and children – lived in close proximity and were therefore able to support each other. I saw these replaced by high-rise flats, often separated within the same building by lifts one of which went to the odd numbered storeys and the other to the even. As a result few neighbours met each other and, in nervousness of dark corridors and the increase of 'mugging', the older people no longer went out at night. This isolation was increased by a change in housing policy by which the different generations no longer lived near each other.

In villages and even in small towns the shops have been forced to close because large super-markets have taken their trade; we have all colluded in this by going to these super-markets. No longer is there good public transport between villages and the local town, and so people are now dependent upon the private car. As a result most people go out of the village for social purposes and for work – the countryside is emptied of its true indigenous population and local community life tends to depend upon those from the towns who have moved in and are willing to be involved. When I was a boy and visited the local village in Devon in which my grandparents lived, practically all social life was centred in the village and in the weekly visit to the local market town – everyone knew all about each other, for better or worse! We have certainly gained in privacy but lost in community; for most people community is the more needed, with privacy available when desired rather than forced upon them.

Again Moltmann says truly:

> Modern society is everywhere a centralised society. It has created the great industrial and administrative centres in the conurbations. As a result it has impoverished the local communities and emptied the countryside. The rebuilding of human society will therefore begin with local communities which can be seen and

experienced and will restore to the local communities many functions and tasks which have been centralised ... the same goes for the established church. We have taken mission, ecumenical relationships and *diaconia* from local communities and delegated them to large organisations. This has made the local [church] community poor and passive.[2]

This is very much what has happened to the Church of England. On a structure which for hundreds of years has been based on local parishes of relatively small communities there has been imposed in this century a massive bureaucratic synodical edifice on a hierarchical basis – General Synod, Diocesan Synod, Deanery Synod – each with its three tiers of bishops, clergy and laity and with an implied leadership from top to bottom rather than the reverse.

Dioceses are usually far too large, so that the bishop becomes a remote figure seen only on official liturgical occasions. The urban parish too is usually so large in population that there is no way in which the whole parish can become a community, and the clergy will certainly never be known by the whole population however hard they attempt to visit. A parish of twenty thousand people can be as impersonal and uncaring as a political and civic area which through its size has become anonymous.

In such a parish a vicar and two curates, or perhaps a team ministry of clergy will try to make sense of their relationship to a parish where they will never know on a personal basis more than a small fraction of the people.

The village parish, on the other hand, which once was a compact unit, is now usually joined with several other villages and the unfortunate priest finds himself on Sundays running from church to church to minister to small groups of people.

The importance of synods grows with their size from P.C.C. (parochial church council) to Deanery Synod, Diocesan Synod and General Synod, but opinion from the grass roots becomes less and less important in influencing decisions taken at the higher levels.

Large-scale organisation has also had an effect on the way the clergy see their duties. In large city parishes the old-style personal approach of the visiting parson has become impossible, and this attitude has spread even to village parishes where it would be still possible for the clergyman to maintain valuable personal relationship with those outside the church as well as those within it. In the area of West Sussex in which I live, not one of the clergy in the surrounding villages is known as a regular visitor of his people. Many say that they have not time to visit, nor to be members of pastoral support groups on a regular basis, yet it is difficult to know in that case how they spend their time, since in country areas there are not great numbers of weekday services, weddings or funerals.

It does seem that in all areas much more time is spent these days on committees and at meetings – the bureaucracy of secular government has been copied by the church. When I was on the General Synod the mass of paper which descended on me before each meeting took many valuable hours to read, time which could have been better spent on being with people. And I never knew how parish clergy from the north of England could spend the time needed for the constant travelling, which many committees held in London demanded of them, without neglecting their parishes.

As a result of present structures much mission and ecumenical work, as Moltmann says, has now been delegated to large organisations and specialists rather than being a natural task of the local community. As a norm now we have diocesan specialists in almost every field of mission evangelism, training both lay and clergy. Mission and evangelism is often seen as something which has to be organised on a vast scale, like a Billy Graham campaign or the Decade of Evangelism. There is, of course, a point in having one person or a group who will focus the work throughout an area like a diocese or sometimes nationally, but Moltmann is right in saying that this often makes the local community 'poor and passive', in that often it waits to be told what to do from the centre rather than getting on with the job from its own local knowledge. I seem to remember a Roman Catholic poster that went something like this: 'God did not save mankind by forming a committee', but if God did not choose this method his churches often have!

If in promoting community and support we are working to fulfil our needs within the framework of reality, then it is quite clear that to create the community of love which is the proper function of the church there needs to be opportunities for reasonably deep knowledge of each other – 'warts and all' – and such knowledge can come only from personal encounter with each other. Where such personal encounter does not happen naturally, there needs to be active enabling of small-scale meetings on a regular basis. Later I will consider how that can be done.

1 Jurgen Moltmann, *Creating a Just Future* (SCM Press 1989), p. 9.
2 Ibid., pp. 9, 10.

12

TRAINING AND REALITY

As I look back and look to the present, one reality which stands out is the wide disparity between the training of the clergy and that of the laity, and the little communication which seems to exist between them. The clergy, whether trained in residential or non-residential courses, are given a fairly rigorous course in the Bible, both Old Testament and New, its origins, discrepancies, conditioning factors, and the motivations and intentions of the respective authors over a period of several thousand years. They are also trained in the origins and growth of church doctrine, the history of the church through the ages, the study and application of Christian ethics and the development of liturgy and spirituality. The laity, on the other hand – despite their more important work of making direct communication of their theological beliefs into the world in which they live and work – receive little training in theology save that which is handed out to them from the pulpit Sunday by Sunday. Just a few may have volunteered for some systematic course of lay training, but otherwise the only training received by the laity has been in confirmation classes when they were young and perhaps later through study groups, if they join them, and the parish magazine, if it is made a vehicle for theological education.

THE RECRUITMENT AND TRAINING OF CLERGY

The gaps which I discovered between the preaching and the practice of many parish clergymen led me to question whether the kind of training we offer, and the method of

selecting professional leaders for the church, have any connection with the reality of their tasks.

Why is it that many of those who come into the ministry
from a wide experience of industrial or professional life so
often not only leave that life behind but also seem to abandon all the experience which could make them into valuable
'bridgers' of the gap between the secular world and the
religious world, and become 'parish pump' men limiting
their vision and task to those within the local congregation?
Why also do clergy whose training – faulty as it is in many
ways – at least gives them a means of critical analysis and
searching of theological truth, so often fall back in their
preaching and teaching on simplistic and moralistic terms
with little regard for what they were taught?

One of the main difficulties in recruiting to the clergy
people with qualities of leadership is that most of the ordi-
nands come from church congregations where they have
been much absorbed in church activities and little in political and social action outside the churches. Thus the kind of
person who finds security in the world of the church then
becomes the local leader ready to perpetuate the 'churchy'
world. The whole procedure becomes self-perpetuating
rather than stimulating to new thinking and action related
to the world outside the church. A writer in *Trust*, a newsletter of the SCM Press, comments:

> I believe there has been a sort of 'brain death' away
> from the churches – many gifted people who would
> have become leaders in the church have ended up by
> leaving it or else giving it little importance in their lives.
> I find that the church has the story which explains and
> inspires my actions and life-style, but I regard as my
> companions those outside the church who are involved
> in political and social action, while those within the
> churches tend to believe and practise the very opposite.

How then is the extensive technical theological training
of the clergy to be linked to the practical life of the laity?
Presumably it is meant to be by communicating this theological and ethical training in terms which are applicable to the
further communication of that training in the world of lay

politics, work, professional and family life – the normal 'context of the text', as Moltmann puts it. But what in reality happens in most parishes?

As I have already pointed out, many of the clergy seem to put aside quickly the technical knowledge of theology gained from their theological college. As *Faith in the City* reports:

> The knowledge so painfully acquired was left behind as soon as the active ministry began; books were sold or left gathering dust upon the shelf. Sermons were written from one well-tried commentary and pastoral methods were learned by rule of thumb. There are thousands of clergy today whose bookshelves as much as their style of ministry are clear evidence that the theological training has borne little fruit in their life's work.[1]

It may also be that the priest becomes submerged by parish life, so that reading and further study often slip out of his life and the text itself is also forgotten. A little diet of literalism and conventional morality takes its place – the laity are then fed with milk, and watery milk at that, instead of strong meat.

So why is it that the clergy quickly even lose what theological expertise they have learnt? One reason is that most of the training at college has been in academic theological research. When the newly ordained clergy come into the parishes it seems to them that such research is going to be of little interest to the laity and do very little for their own personal lives. So they give it up. Then, since there has been little training in relating text to context and the whole prophetic understanding of theology has, from the fear of interfering in politics, been played down, such teaching as the clergy give often amounts to little more than pietistic moralism or dogmatic fundamentalism. Apart from the teachings of liberation theology there has been little understanding that faith and action must go together and that there should be no closed areas for theological reflection.

'Christian faith is not understood by the intellectual acceptance of the words of a doctrinal formulation but by taking the risk of faith in action,' says Ronald Preston.[2] But clerical training has shown little understanding of the thought of liberation theologians, like Juan Luis Segundo, who holds that theology must start from a commitment to change and to improve the world.

Moreover, we Anglicans have been influenced by the consciousness that ours is an established church, and so the average preacher does not see himself as a member of a creative minority within the world, committed to human struggle for the poor and for justice and freedom, but rather as one who, within a conventional and largely conservative society, must not 'rock the boat'. Yet within such a society it is the preacher who *does* see himself as speaking from theological reflection upon the realities of our world who receives attention and motivates thinking. In my Surrey parish, and now in West Sussex, both of which areas are noted for their political and religious conservatism, I find it is my most challenging and controversial sermons for which I receive requests for transcripts and then later have real hard-hitting, thought-provoking debate.

LACK OF TRAINING FOR THE LAITY

If the sole education of the laity is to be through the sermon, and the sermon consists of notes hastily thrown together late on a Saturday evening and made with an assumption that – despite what was learnt during the years of study – each text from the Bible is simply to be taken at its face value, then it is not surprising if the laity find little in it that relates to their complex and often difficult working and civic life.

So, despite the great need in the present world for a strongly educated laity to extend the work of relating theology to life, there is little evidence of systematic education for them. For a short period of six weeks during Lent a small minority of the congregation may meet week by week to study a commended book or some diocesan or national scheme. But there it will end, and even such groups will vary widely in value. One of my ex-parishioners, a highly intelligent, retired headmistress, attended a parish study group in expectation of learning through mutual discussion, only to find there just the vicar and three elderly ladies – the vicar held forth rather vaguely for an hour and the three ladies fell asleep!

Occasionally from on high comes some grand scheme for theological education and mission – for example, the present Decade of Evangelism – but in most parishes all that happens are some rather general and vague plans that quickly die, and things remain much as before. Very rarely in any parish is there any systematic theological education relating text to context as a normal and regular part of parish life and work throughout the year and involving most of the church membership.

There is also a widespread lack of interest by the laity even in what little is provided for them by way of continuing education. One reason is that many of the current theological concerns of the church are of little interest to the laity, who are not primarily interested either in academic theology or in the excessive concern in some sections of the church with issues of personal sexual morality. Moreover, they also suspect that a church geared to a ministerial hierarchy does not really want them to show too much interest in its government or in its power structures – these being the concern primarily of the clergy, the laity being expected to accept them. Don Cupitt refers to this:

> There has been much enthusiasm for the theology of the laity. But it is quite certain that the laity will be upgraded in the church only so far as the process does not diminish the traditional powers of the clergy . . . since very early times there have been two Christianities, one for the clergy and one for the laity. For the priest who is a stipendiary professional, the church is a centred power structure and he is one of the power élite. By contrast the lay person, being powerless, has a religion of love, reconciliation and reliance for strength upon God and the fortifying ministrations of her church.[3]

The situation regarding lay training seems also – despite Ruth Etchells's words quoted in the Tiller Report (and in chapter 3 here) – to have developed towards a more churchy associational basis than a communal extensive character. In the Tiller Report these two concepts of the church were described.[4] In the *communal church* 'distinction between membership of the church and membership of the community is vague or non-existent'; the communal church might be that which is usually understood by the term 'C. of E.' on official forms and in the sense that everyone in England lives in a parish of the established church and has rights of baptism, marriage and funeral. The *associational church* is one in which 'people subscribe to a particular set of doctrinal formulations and are prepared to meet the necessary demands of such membership'. Membership in this kind of church probably implies an act of disassociation from the values of the community and an accompanying sense of mission, not to change the community as such, but to persuade other individuals to transfer their interests and allegiance to the church as an alternative community. Neither type of church sees the training of its people to be for mission or ministry for service in the secular world. The communal church all too easily becomes a loosely knit 'club' offering its services to all and sundry but not expecting anyone to take commitment too seriously; the associational church trains its members for a committed ministry but within the church rather than to the world. In neither case is training seen as relating text to context in terms of the needs of society. In both types of church those who belong will be trained as functioning members within the church rather than as catalysts within society.

In this connection Kenneth Leech has written:

> ... the normal condition of the church in society is that of a creative minority, as indicated by the symbolism of leaven. The purpose of leaven is not to transform the whole piece of dough into leaven but into bread. This view has widespread pastoral implications where the Church of England is being forced to a decision as to whether it sees itself as a national church spokesman of a mainstream religious culture, as it is in law, or a small potentially creative minority, as it is in fact.[5]

If his view is correct, as I think it is, then neither the

communal nor the associational church offers the kind of training which enables the lay person to see himself or herself as part of a non-conforming 'creative minority' within society and to accept both the difficulties and the opportunities involved in such a vision of lay service.

It can be seen then that the clergy are, in the words of Don Cupitt, a 'power élite' and are trained to that end; the laity are a dependent ministry and, being dependent, are dealt out the kind of training and education which augments the power of the church and does not challenge it too greatly. The result is again clearly seen by Cupitt: ' . . . the hierarchs do not wish to give up their power and the laity do not wish to give up their weakness, and it is hard to tell which need, the need for power or the need for weakness, is the greater.'[6]

What then happens? The person who has taken the trouble to study the needs of the world around him or her and is willing to enter into the necessary power struggles of that world is more often found outside the church. The local church becomes a small and ineffectual group of people and the local priest enjoys being a power-figure to a group who will never count for much in the neighbourhood. His power, therefore, becomes as ineffectual as theirs and both he and they are largely ignored when important decisions have to be made in the locality or in the wider world.

1 Report of the Archbishop of Canterbury's Commission on Urban Priority Areas, *Faith in the City* (1985), p. 120.
2 Ronald Preston, *Future of Christian Ethics* (SCM Press 1987), p. 170.
3 Don Cupitt, *Radicals and the Future of the Church* (SCM Press 1989), p. 72.
4 The Tiller Report, *A Strategy for the Church's Ministry*, General Synod 1983.
5 An article by Kenneth Leech in *Theology*, July 1981.
6 Cupitt, op. cit., p. 72.

13

WORSHIP AND REALITY

There is a great dilemma when trying to reconcile present methods of worship with that which the worship is trying to express. It has often been said that worship is about worth; through worship we are relating, in symbols, all that means worth in our own lives to all that means worth to God.

Robin Green in his very valuable book on worship, *Only Connect*, sums up his many important illustrations through dream, story and role play of the connection between worship and life:

> What I have tried to demonstrate is that there is a key connection between how the symbols are mediated in worship and the growth of people. Worship, by its very nature, cares for people because it creates a matrix within which both our individuality and our sociality can grow.[1]

But it is very difficult to bring this out realistically through any of our recognised forms of liturgical worship, as Robin Green himself has discovered. I once preached in his church in Earls Court and found that the worship there was very like the worship anywhere else. This was no fault of his, but it showed how a congregation allergic to change can successfully resist any innovative attitudes to traditional worship however good. Later Robin Green found that he could not express his priesthood through worship and had to give up functioning as a leader of eucharistic worship.

As I look at the worship offered in the various kinds of Anglican church I find that in each one there is, amidst what is good, more that is missing. As I have already mentioned, the charismatic evangelicals offer a kind of community but one that is very inbred, also the use of the body in worship and a certain joyfulness of spirit in song and forms of music, but these are often of second-rate quality. There is too a lack of a sense of transcendence, and the mind is prostituted by an unintelligent use of Scripture. The Anglo-Catholics offer a sense of beauty and of tradition, the dignity of ceremony and some feeling of mystery and awe, but they express little relationship between life and liturgy and between liturgy and the dynamic prophetic action that Kenneth Leech envisages:

> ... the idea of liturgy is closely linked to that of drama; it is a celebratory event in which something is expected to happen. The liturgy of the Eucharist is thus a deeply subversive act, a spiritual force working within the fallen world to undermine it and renew it.[2]

I worship regularly in Anglo-Catholic churches, but I should be hard put to it to describe what goes on there as a 'deeply subversive act'!

If I go outside the Anglican Church I find the same: in Baptist churches the same virtues and faults of evangelical fundamentalism; in other non-conformist churches a kind of 'hymn-sandwich' service led entirely by the minister and lacking either beauty or form. In Roman Catholic churches I shall probably find a liturgy subject to similar faults of populism as the Alternative Service Book and without the colourful ceremonial which at one time pleased at least the senses if not the mind. In no group save the Society of Friends shall I find that connection between silence and social solidarity which helps me realise that, in the words of T. S. Eliot, 'The desert is in the heart of your brother'.[3] The poet R. S. Thomas captures the emptiness of the desert of contemporary worship which is actually experienced, when he writes in his poem 'The Empty Church':

> ... Why, then, do I kneel still
> striking my prayers on stone
> heart? Is it in hope one
> of them will ignite yet and throw

> on its illumined walls the shadow
> of someone greater than I can understand?[4]

And Monica Furlong's description of religion in general is particularly true of much public worship:

> What has disappeared is the old sense of the creativity of religion, liberating, releasing, making men joyful, helping them to grow. Christianity appears a tired religion, dog-eared round the edges, talking in tired language, shrinking from bold thought and courageous new ideas.[5]

Religious worship is tending to degenerate in two directions:

1. For some it becomes a private cult by which the individual may retreat from the world – hence in worship the emphasis on the 'early' communion as a private affair between a woman and her God. For others it provides a secure ghetto of superficial community and happiness in an insecure world, a traditional ritual beauty and appeal to the senses related more to the past than to the present or future, or just an interesting intellectualism speaking more to an Oxbridge common room than to the streets of south London.

2. Sometimes religious worship is used as a means to an end – a useful way of maintaining respect for authority, law and order, custom and tradition and private morality. School assembly is looked upon by many as a means of moral indoctrination and the church, as I have previously remarked, has all too readily gone down this path of private morality.

Worship thought of as an incentive to law and order or as a way of maintaining morality soon becomes either associated for ever with authority or judged as to its effectuality by its capacity to 'make us good'. Already this has all too often become the criterion by which public worship is assessed; how often have I and many other priests heard the comment, 'I can be good without coming to church', or, 'I don't go to church because the people who do are better than I am.' But how dull this makes worship, since 'being good' for many means no more than observing the conventional precepts of morality. I cannot imagine that an average young person today feels any urge to join public worship because it will 'make him or her good', nor can I understand why any schoolteacher would imagine that children who are bored with religion will find the indoctrination of morality any more exciting. When religion, church and worship are considered only from the standpoint of their expediency and usefulness for other reasons, then they are bound to vanish as soon as the purposes of society can be served by other means. As Bonhoeffer once said, 'If we have a God of the gaps in life, then what happens when all the gaps have been filled?'

So if worship is looked upon as a means to an end other than as an end in itself it will always fail. If religion does not have meaning and value in itself, then it has no purpose or meaning at all. A religion which has to justify itself by its social or ethical value or its moral usefulness is not only extremely dull but has no capacity for joy or hope within it that could not equally be validated by the social services or by psychotherapy.

How then do we change worship from being just a means of imposing morality or providing an alternative world to that in which we live? In other words, how do we make worship not a world apart but the reflection and anticipation of a world to come – a world which could be, as the poet says, 'ignited by God'? Somehow this expectation of what worship means has to be set forth in many different ways in order to connect with the varying capacity and understanding of worshippers.

Writing in *Theology* an Anglican priest in south London observed:

> There can be no assembly without the call of God which is a matter of present experience, not past remembrance. The church only knows itself in the worship of God . . . But the life which is celebrated in the assembly of the elect is not one of those redeemed from the

69

world. Their worship is meant to be a foretaste of the joy to come for all creation.[6]

This is on the same line of thinking as that of Moltmann who, in his book *The Open Church*, speaks of the liturgy as an act of joy and liberation, an act in which the age which is to come – the age of the kingdom of God – is celebrated in anticipation.

But how difficult it is to express this thinking which is, I am convinced, the true aim and purpose of worship – namely, the transformation of society, rather than separation from it, through forms of worship. It certainly involves a far more radical change than simply altering the words and form of existing liturgy. For example, the change in the Church of England from the 1662 Prayer Book to the Alternative Service Book, with its Rites A and B, appears to have done nothing to increase the appeal of Anglican worship; the churches are still relatively empty. And the absence of a set liturgy in the so-called Free Churches seems to have no greater appeal.

We have to consider not just changes to institutional worship but rather a radical rethinking of the many different ways in which community and assembly can be expressed so that, in the words of John Robinson, 'Holy Communion can be an expression of holy community.' Difficult as it is, it would be cowardice on my part not to attempt to look into possibilities for the future drawn from my own experiences of both past and present, and that I shall do in chapter 25.

1 Robin Green, *Only Connect* (Darton, Longman and Todd 1987), p. 132.
2 Kenneth Leech, *True God* (Sheldon Press 1985), p. 291.
3 T.S. Eliot, Choruses from 'The Rock', *Selected Poems*, Faber 1964.
4 R.S. Thomas, *Later Poems 1972–1982* (Macmillan 1983), p. 113.
5 Monica Furlong, *With Love to the Church* (Hodder and Stoughton 1965), p. 24.
6 Christopher Moody, in an article in *Theology* (March/April 1991), p. 88.

14

SPIRITUALITY AND REALITY

When I was Director of Lay Training in the Diocese of Southwark and attending one of our conferences on spirituality, a young man cried out somewhat angrily after a long discussion on prayer: 'I don't want to be taught how to say my prayers. What I want to be taught is the far more difficult question – how do I pray my life? What does praying my life mean?'

Spirituality in its widest sense is just that – learning how to pray my life. In other words, how do I become what I am meant to be: namely, made in the image of God and incarnating that image in the words and actions of my daily life?

In my book *Prayer in a Secular City* I tried to answer that young man's question. I also quoted there from a Roman Catholic Dominican, Father Besnard:

> The spirituality sought by the Christian is a spirituality to be lived. The language with which God speaks to man and man to God, is not primarily words but rather daily events, those choices that souls are continually called to make because of their very existence and which the Incarnation has shown us as not only the life of man, but the life of Christ in man and yet no less the life of Christ.[1]

These words accord with those of Kenneth Leech:

> Christian spirituality is about a process of formation, a process in which we are formed by and in Christ . . . it is a process of Christ-ening, of being clothed with Christ, and in this process we are transformed.[2]

71

However, just as there is seen to be an increasing lack of reality in worship as related to life, so also the same is true of spirituality in regard to the life of prayer. Prayer has been seen as something separate from life or as an addition to life, without any particular expectation of its influencing what we do. I give two examples of this. When I was a parish priest I found that it was taken for granted that all meetings of the Parish Church Council would open with prayer. However, in the course of the meeting it was clear that the prayer made no difference at all to the conduct of the meeting. In the discussions we still held firmly to our own opinions and often paid little attention to those of others. In fact, we behaved exactly as we would have done if we had not officially prayed!

The same was true when I attended General Synod: before the great debates, especially those of a controversial nature, we prayed for the guidance of the Holy Spirit, but we knew that we had already made up our minds the way we would speak or vote. If we thought of the guidance of the Holy Spirit at all it was more likely to be that we hoped the Holy Spirit would guide those who differed from us to change their minds. At the risk of seeming cynical I have to say that my impression was that prayer was more part of an official routine than a realistic expectation of change. How far that attitude also penetrates into private and personal prayer it is difficult to judge but, from my own experience and that of many others when they speak honestly, I suspect it does so considerably.

There is also considerable confusion these days about the meaning and effectualness of prayer. The opening of David Hare's play *Racing Demon* has caught well this spirit of religious confusion. The radical but confused priest is praying:

> God, where are you? I wish you would talk to me, God. It isn't just me, there's a general feeling. This is what people are saying in the parish. They want to know where you are. The joke wears thin, you never say anything ... you see it's this perpetual absence – yes? This not being there – it's that – I mean, let's be honest,

it's just beginning to get some of us down. You know? Is that unreasonable? There are an awful lot of people in a very bad way. And they need something besides silence, God. Do you understand?[3]

There is caught here the experience of many. We pray for what seems only good and right, what ordinary human love would see as right – that someone very ill and still young and with much to offer needs healing and new life, or alternatively that someone very old and with nothing left to live for needs death, and in both cases nothing apparently happens. Then we are perplexed, and we say: 'What is wrong with my prayers? Why is God's idea of love and compassion so different from mine? If I am wrong about the meaning of love and its actions then let God tell me so, but he doesn't.' As the vicar in the play experienced, the difficulty is not that God doesn't answer prayer as we would wish but that he doesn't tell us why.

Then we are reduced to making excuses for God. We say God looks at things from eternity not from just earthly living, or that God's healing is not necessarily physical but spiritual, and then we find that there doesn't appear to be any spiritual healing either. We cannot see why having eternal life means that earthly life has to be cut short or made a suffering hell. And so we need to teach ourselves and others to pray our lives, to have a realistic spirituality in which there is carried into the world not my mind but the mind of Christ.

The praying of our lives; the capacity to 'be still and know God', and also to know ourselves; to be able to bear solitude, to be alone without being lonely: these are vitally necessary in a world like ours which makes two assumptions. The first is that we must save the maximum amount of time in travel, in concentration and in labour efficiency, but no one thinks to ask for what purpose the time saved is to be used. Speed has become an end in itself and as a result the restlessness so constantly at work in the human spirit is increased. The second assumption is that activism is far more valuable than passivism and being still.

Oscar Wilde once said: 'In the opinion of the world

contemplation is the gravest sin of which you can be guilty: in the opinion of the highest civilisations it is the proper occupation of man.'

Contemplation requires some powers of concentration, but these days most people lack the ability to concentrate. This shows itself in many different ways: the tabloid newspapers, where headlines, shortness of article and reliance upon gut-reaction rather than sustained thought, all aim deliberately at people who cannot maintain sustained thought and whose attention span is severely limited; in television, programmes are usually divided into short serial slots, and far more time is allotted to programmes which require little thought and only superficial attention than to serious reflective themes. These examples show how the media authorities understand that the majority of human beings have little wish to give sustained attention to anything. Home life also shows this same desire to avoid real communication and serious thinking; the family meal and conversation seem often to have been destroyed by television.

But is the church any better at helping people to be still, to think and reflect? I would say that the church is most unhelpful in enabling people to find stillness. Most churches present their congregations with a hive of activities during the week, and despite the fact that the Alternative Service Book has at stated places in the liturgy the words, 'Silence may be observed here,' this rarely is observed. Activism and desire for speed dominate even churches: we are all constantly encouraged to 'join things'; the service must be over within the hour; the sermon is not judged by its quality but by its quantity. Is it that we are afraid of silence and that the media and the tabloid press have made us incapable of concentration? If so, this is surely something that the church should not accept but help to redress.

Looking then to the future of the church we need to consider how we may bring to reality the words of Kenneth Leech:

> A church should be a place of spiritual nourishment, a power house of spiritual growth . . . the condition of the

desert . . . a place of silence, of attention to God in simplicity and faith – all these should be made accessible in each parish community.[4]

Also it is surely the task of the church to enable people to learn that wisdom which is reflection on the meaning of life and the knowledge of how to use it. Schumacher said in one of his books:

> We are now far too clever to be able to survive without wisdom . . . the higher powers of man, no longer being brought into play to produce the knowledge of wisdom, atrophy and even disappear altogether . . . Efforts become ever more frantic, while unsolved and seemingly insoluble problems accumulate. While wealth may still be accumulating, the quality of man declines.[5]

In a world in which events follow one another with increasing speed and the media constantly pours information into us, we have to pause to ask questions such as, 'What is the purpose and goal of our existence?' 'What are we doing with our world, with our church, with ourselves?' 'What values of life are we communicating if we are to act with sense and without ruining our planet?' If those who claim to follow the Lord of all life and all creation cannot give attention to these questions, then who will?

So far we have been thinking mostly about churchgoers. But what then of all those people who do not claim to follow the Lord of all life, who regard religion as irrelevant in their lives?

Dietrich Bonhoeffer once asked the question: 'What should we do to make Christ become the Lord of the irreligious?' It was he also who said that the real difficulty facing Christianity was not in finding reassurances for those with problems but how to speak with those who had no conscious needs, those for whom life was quite pleasant, who had moderate success in wealth and human relationships and who felt no need for any outside spiritual sustenance.

In fact, there are even some who have been churchgoers

75

who find that cutting their connections with official religion or religious institutions is a relief. I have two friends – one an Anglican and previously a churchwarden in a former parish, the other a lapsed Roman Catholic – both have said how liberated they feel since they have given up any official religious observance. One said: 'I feel like someone released from prison'; the other said: 'It is like leaving a home of rules and regulations which not only do not fit me but even hinder my fulfilment as a free person.'

In my experience over fifty years I have to admit that I have not found the answer to Bonhoeffer's question and neither has the official church. If enthusiasm for religion is to be measured by attendance at churches, then, apart from those churches which seem to attract numbers by what I can only call the pseudo-security and inbred community of a highly emotional and irrational fundamentalism, there has not only been a steady decline in churchgoing but an increasing number who have never in their lives had any connection whatever with any religious group.

Such people – the 'irreligious' of Bonhoeffer's question – now form the majority of the population in this country. They find the secular consumerist, wealth-creating type of society encouraged by the Conservative government since 1979 quite satisfactory, at least so long as life brings no major crises and, even then, they would not look for outside supernatural help. I am not talking here about the conscious atheist or the intellectual agnostic. (Indeed, when I meet them I often find common ground, since we are both interested in religion.) Nor am I referring to lapsed Christians; there are many of these, but at least their original upbringing or background of faith shows itself from time to time, either through what we call 'folk religion' or at times of crisis.

We are then usually dealing as much with those who are completely indifferent and have been untouched by religion throughout their lives as with lapsed Christians. An example remains in my mind. When I was vicar of Camberwell I had as a lodger a young man, intelligent and friendly, who – with considerable courage, I thought – lived for three years in a vicarage directly opposite the church and entered it only once, for a concert. He told me that never in his life had he had anything to do with religion, nor did he ever think it likely that he would. (This is true. When I met him recently after twenty years he was still utterly indifferent to anything religious.) He told me that when he was a small boy his mother had said to him, 'If you are naughty, I shall send you to Sunday School', and he made sure he never was that naughty. His views on worship were forcibly expressed: 'I can't think why at 9.30 on a Sunday morning, when all civilised people are in bed, anybody should want to sit for an hour on hard seats in that cold and draughty church to listen to you!' I had to admit that, if that was all that worship was, I couldn't understand it either! But of the twenty thousand people who lived in Camberwell I should think David represented the attitude of the vast majority.

As far as most people are concerned the question of God no longer arises. When confronted directly with the question, 'Do you believe in God?' they may hesitate to reply with a definite 'No', but for all practical and living purposes, the non-relevance of God is accepted as a normal state of affairs fully consonant with what modern man sees as reasonable. If there is any kind of unconscious philosophy today it is a crude kind of existentialism, by which I mean a concentration upon the concerns of the present moment. According to one notable existentialist, Heidegger, man is a being confronted by death and his problem is to find a significant existence in the face of this limitation. But for most people that significant existence does not include much consideration of religion. It might also be said that present attitudes are summed up in the comment that, for most people, it doesn't matter what you believe so long as you believe it doesn't matter. A comment in the *Independent* in 1989 enlarged on this attitude:

As religious belief has died away there has been no corresponding growth in religious disbelief: professing atheists are a small minority. What has flourished is what one might call irreligious belief: a recent IBA survey showed that 74 per cent of the population claim to believe that Jesus is the Son of God, only 62 per cent

77

believe that God created the universe, and 70 per cent believe that no one church or faith can be the only true religion.[6]

What appears to have happened is that religious language has lost all agreed meaning, so that people are able to assent to all sorts of contradictory propositions without noticing anything odd. Not only is Britain no longer a Christian country; it has become one in which Christianity is almost impossible for most people to imagine. If it means anything to the general public, it means a code of sexual morality which is no longer enforced by law or followed by the majority. Another writer to the *Independent* commented:

> Because people are uninterested, the Church of England is dying. Apathy threatens to destroy it. A fatal gap is opening between those who take Christianity very seriously indeed and those who couldn't care less. The former are a small minority. Like obsessive people in any field, they are not always good at understanding the point of view of those untouched by their zeal![7]

Unless, however, it is to be accepted that Christianity is only meant to be a sect, accepted or rejected like any other group such as Jehovah's Witnesses or Scientology, then somehow those untouched by the minority cannot be left untouched. I said earlier, I have not found the answer to Bonhoeffer's question, but I hope to show later, from my experience, some ways which might lead to an answer if the church is genuinely seeking one. That may sound a little cynical, but I sometimes think that many within the church are quite happy to go on being members of a club that caters for their tastes without being much concerned for those who show no desire to join.

1 Father Besnard, in an article in *Concilium*, vol. 9, no. 1.
2 Kenneth Leech, *Spirituality and Pastoral Care* (Sheldon Press 1986), p. 5.
3 David Hare, *Racing Demon*, Faber 1991.

4 Leech, op. cit., p. 27.
5 E.F. Schumacher, *A Guide for the Perplexed* (Jonathan Cape 1977), p. 67.
6 Andrew Brown, in an article in the *Independent*, December 1989.
7 Andrew Gimson, in an article in the *Independent*, August 1989.

Part Three

LOOKING TO THE FUTURE

15

A MODEL FOR THE CHURCH

The time has now come for me to let the past speak to the future. Here I find an ambivalence in my hopes for the future of the Anglican Church. On the one hand, I see the church which in ordinary circumstances seems to make little or no impact on the lives and attitudes of people; in most areas it is represented by a comparatively small group of mostly older people meeting once a week, and perhaps occasionally during the week, for religious services or meetings, and is ignored by the vast majority of people in the parish except for weddings and funerals. On the other hand, I am also aware that this same church attracts a considerable amount of attention in the media, that its leaders are often interviewed and quoted, that the views of General Synod are not entirely ignored by politicians and that many of the serious newspapers from time to time make religious and ethical issues the subject of leading articles. In fact, the public face of the church is often much more than would be expected, judging by the numbers who regularly attend it.

I would want, therefore, this public face to be far more reflected in the influence which Christians have on the area around them. The rest of this book will be concerned with suggestions as to how this could be so. In the various fields of theology, sexuality, community, church, structure, training, worship and spirituality, I shall be guided by two criteria: the reality of the situation (not some 'ideal', but the actual context in which we are working) and a theology which stresses the creative rather than the negative, a gospel which emphasises more the 'thou shalt' than the 'thou shalt not'. Love of the good rather than fear of the bad is what helps most on the journey towards fulfilment and liberation

in life. I shall deal fully and in detail with the various areas
of life, as I do not want wishful thinking or remote ideas to
take the place of constructive analysis leading to practical
action.

It is always good to have a model by which a church of
the future may be assessed. A few years ago I was very
impressed by a model given by the then Bishop of Win-
chester, John Taylor, in a lecture at St George's House, Wind-
sor. He called the lecture 'A Church Reshaped' and he used
three models for the future well-being of the church. The
first was based upon the work of a pioneer doctor in psychiatric work in hospitals, both in England and overseas, who
promoted open meetings between staff and patients in
which there could be complete freedom of criticism
together with the enabling of both groups to reveal their
own anxieties, fears and insecurities. This is a practice which
has been adopted also in many Christian and non-Christian
communes in various parts of the world; these communes
operate on the basis of a shared and open supportive life.
A leader of such a community described it as a model for
the church:

> It has seemed to me that our greatest need is not for
> more 'evangelism' but for the development of insti-
> tutions as centres of living fellowship, where the essence
> of the Gospel communicates itself by virtue of its total
> atmosphere and environment. This means that the all-
> accepting nature of God's attitude to us is made real by
> a similar quality of fearless and forgiving relationships
> within the community. We all feel the need of deeper
> fellowship and strive hard to be 'nice' and loving to
> each other. This, however, often ignores the fact that it
> cannot be done by denying those aspects of our lives
> which are against such attitudes.[1]

The second model came from the need for church congregations in one of the most secularised societies in Europe,
the then German Democratic Republic, to find ways by
which they could ask fundamental questions about the
values and needs of the society in which they found themselves living. Just attending church and listening to sermons

was of little value; just being outwardly Christian on Sundays and colluding with the secular society on weekdays simply led to a life divided between two philosophies of living. So the congregations set up seminars on various questions of importance, particularly in regard to education, which would enable questions to be asked which, while not directly subversive, questioned the values of secularist views of achievement.

The third model showed how a church in Hong Kong had, by making itself aware of the needs of the poor and oppressed in the area, organised itself effectively, using the processes of protest and action available to it, in order to achieve better conditions for the people of the area.

On the basis of these three models John Taylor says:

> Between them they present all the essential features of a church engaged in the Christian mission. All three models have to do with proclaiming Christ. But each exemplifies a different method. Equally, all these models show the fellowship of the redeemed community working upon its members. But each represents a different form of that fellowship. One is a therapeutic fellowship in which each member learns to be fearlessly open to the rest and so gives and receives healing and support. The second is an interpretative fellowship in which the members help each other to reflect on some aspect of their human situation in the light of their faith, in order to have questions to ask and insights to share with other people. The third is a dynamically responsible fellowship which enables its members to rise to their full human potential and to engage positively in changing that area of the world's life for which, under God, they take responsibility.[2]

These seem to me very comprehensive models which could be used to guide and assess thinking for the church of the future. They could be summarised as a SUPPORTIVE CHURCH, a THINKING CHURCH and a RESPONSIBLE AND ACTIVE CHURCH. It is the unity and harmony of these activities of a church that make it effectively, in the words of St Paul, 'the Body of Christ'. If any of the three is lacking, or is being inadequately carried out, the work of the church and its effectiveness are weakened: 'Bonded and knit together by every constituent joint, the whole frame grows through the due activity of each part, and builds itself up in love' (Ephesians 4:16).

In the following chapters, in which I write of how I would like to see the church being and acting in relation to different aspects of its life and work, I shall be bearing in mind these three models, as well as following the two criteria I have outlined: namely, reality in regard to the situation and a theology which is creative and thus helps the church towards fulfilling its work. I must, of course, immediately qualify this by saying that, since what I write arises from my own experience, I shall be concerned mainly with the church to which I belong: namely, the established Church of England.

1 John V. Taylor, *A Church Reshaped*, CMS 1975.
2 Ibid.

16

A THINKING CHURCH

THE RELATION OF THEOLOGY TO LIFE

The first necessity in the communication of a theology related to life is to be able to acknowledge what are the realities of life and then to be able to see how a God of love is with us as we face those realities. Bonhoeffer rightly says:

> Action which is in accordance with Christ is action which is in accordance with reality. This proposition is not an ideal demand, but it is an assertion which springs from the knowledge of reality itself . . . action which is in accordance with Christ is in accordance with reality because it allows the world to be the world; it reckons with the world as the world; and yet it never forgets that in Jesus Christ the world is loved, condemned and reconciled by God.

But he also states firmly that:

> God is not a reassuring background music to my life. God is not a buttress to shore up the contradictions of existence. The only God who can be of any value to me in the world of real life is the God who shares the reality with me and does not even try to protect me from it.[1]

In chapter 9 I wrote of the unreality of some religious groups whose attraction is in their offering, in this insecure world, a comfortable charismatic club to those who accept their teachings. Kenneth Leech describes this false security in the following words:

> There is a false peace which comes not from rootedness

87

in God but from a kind of analgesic spirituality which seeks to remove the pains and conflicts both of the world and of the heart by dulling the consciousness. Marx correctly identified much religion as the opium of the people; today it would be more correct to see much spirituality as the religious equivalent of Librium and Valium . . . the provision of opium for the people is not the purpose of the pastoral ministry.[2]

All this comes from a misunderstanding of the doctrine of the love of God, a misunderstanding with which the church has often colluded by trying to provide a comfortable and undisturbing religion and by its insistence that there are orthodox answers which can be laid on from above. Then, when the answers do not fit the reality, there is disillusionment and scepticism about the whole value of Christian belief, or indeed any other 'orthodoxies' which claim to meet any and every situation.

Much of the confusion between reality and so-called religious answers arises from a denial of the true theology of the cross. We have seen a church which sets up in every building the cross as its symbol of faith, but it is usually a jewelled cross, a cross which speaks nothing to the reality of the pain of human beings and speaks even less to the actual life of the church in which it is centrally placed. We have preached for generations a God of love and we have rightly done so, but in that preaching we have fallen into great difficulties, due often to our misunderstanding of the nature of love. Because we think more of the gratifications than of the vulnerability of love, we find it difficult to cope with situations in which our understanding of God's love appears to be defeated: we see evil flourishing in all parts of the world; there is an excess of violence, injustice and abuse which seems to grow rather than diminish; or someone whom we have loved and cared for is reduced by a stroke or by Alzheimer's Disease from a witty, vivacious human being to a mindless, vacant, semi-alive shadow of himself or herself. Then, when we want to be able to speak of the wisdom of old age, we are confronted instead with the reality of the incontinence, withdrawal and helplessness of the geri-

88

atric ward or the creeping senility of one who has lived too long, but does not actually, in physical terms, die. We speak of the qualities of meekness, simplicity of life and humility, but in reality it is those who exhibit none of those qualities who prosper in our world, and we cry with the psalmist: 'Lord, how long shall the ungodly triumph?'

Yes, time and time again we seem to see in the world that which, according to our own understanding of love, has no meaning, no purpose, no gain either for the victims or for those who care for them. We speak of useless pain, useless anguish, and we ask: 'Why, Lord, why?' – and usually we receive no answer. Then again we are giving scope to the enemies of religion to cry: 'How can you believe in a God of love when such things happen?' – we are supposed to have answers. We try to explain away the God of unanswered prayer, of innocent suffering, and our explanations ring hollow even to ourselves. So great is our inborn belief, even as Christians, that life is meant to be happy – a pleasure garden, the original Eden before the Fall.

This is where it is not so much our idea of God as a God of love which is wrong as the unreality of our thoughts when we use the word 'love'. Love at its deepest level is not the 'love' which can be shown only when all things go well with me, when life is easy and happy and at its pleasantest. Even love at the real human level is not like that. The deepest love is shown not when I pray that those I love may be released from suffering, but when I pray to be allowed to enter into and share that suffering.

There is a story which I think comes from Kafka, but I cannot trace its origin. A woman, to her intense pain, heard judgement delivered upon her son at his death, and he for his misdoings was sent to hell. She in her pain and grief battered on the doors of hell, crying, 'Let him out.' The doors remained firmly shut. At last, wearied with crying and realising the uselessness of her cries she battered again, but this time she cried: 'Let me in.' The doors were then opened to her. Love at its deepest level does not cry 'Let me (or let her) out of the worlds of pain and misery', but it is the love which cries, 'Let me in'. That is the God of love in whom we believe, the God who is crucified, as we also are sometimes crucified.

As Moltmann and Bonhoeffer so vividly stress – the former in *The Crucified God* and the latter through his personal experience of crucifixion in *Letters and Papers from Prison* – the God who loves us is the God who allows himself to be driven to the cross. This is a concept of love which is utterly alien to our Western world with its emphasis on happy and successful living. The God who loves us is the God who wills to go into hell that we might live. The God who loves us is the God who in the hell which we have made of her world* does not stand aside from that hell, but becomes one with it and dies with us when we kill ourselves.

Perhaps the most vivid illustration of this is to be seen in the scourge of AIDS. The God who is love does not, like so many religious people, condemn those who in their natural love of the pleasures of sex have crucified themselves, but rather hugs the contaminated body of the AIDS victim and allows herself to touch, to kiss, to be there as a 'buddy'. The God who is love is the God who is incontinent with the incontinent, helpless with the helpless, weak with the weak, oppressed with the oppressed – never separated. It is just because we know she is there that we can bear the humiliation, the suffering. It is just because the cross has shown us that kind of God, that we know without her we are lost; we do not expect release from the pain but we do know she is with us in the pain. Bonhoeffer puts this exactly:

> God lets himself be pushed out of the world on to the cross. He is weak and powerless in the world, and that is precisely the way, the only way, in which he is with us and helps us. Matthew 8:17 ['he took away our diseases from us and carried our diseases for us'] makes it quite clear that Christ helps us, not by virtue of his omnipotence, but by virtue of his weakness and suffering . . .

* Throughout this section I have used both him and her to designate God in order to show: (a) that God is truly neither, but spirit; (b) that nevertheless God as revealed in Christ is not male or female, but both male and female in personal attributes.

only the suffering God can help ... That is a reversal of what the religious man expects from God. Man is summoned to share in God's suffering at the hands of a godless world.[3]

It is false religion which is constantly feeling thwarted when God's supposed omnipotence does not immediately bring help, when asked for, to relieve pain and suffering. In Moltmann's profound words: 'In the forsakenness of the Son the Father also forsakes himself. In the surrender of the Son the Father also surrenders himself, though not in the same way.'[4] The different way is that the Father suffers in the death of the Son, in that infinite suffering which is the true grief of love when there is the sense of forsakenness. The Son experiences dying in forsakenness but not ultimate death, because the suffering presupposes the life which is to be the vindication of the suffering.

It should not really have been difficult for the church to understand what is meant by the love of God in relation to powerlessness rather than power, to weakness rather than success, to the anguish of life rather than superficial happiness, since it is shown clearly in both the gospels and the epistles, especially in the words of St Paul:

> For the foolishness of God is wiser than men, and the weakness of God is stronger than men ... God chose what is foolish in the world to shame the wise, God chose what is weak in the world to shame the strong, God chose what is low and despised in the world, even things that are not, to bring to nothing things that are. (1 Corinthians 1:25, 27–8 RSV)

But so strongly rooted in the Western world is the idea that life should be successful, that prosperity and power are to be encouraged – and particularly has this been the philosophy of the USA and of Thatcherite Britain – that the church has colluded with this view of life, not for the first time in its history. Modern politics has welcomed the market economy as the answer to all economic problems, despite three million unemployed; modern religion has welcomed a religion of large charismatic groups – always looking happy, clapping and waving hands, spelling out the idea that life is for happiness and Christ is a kind of cheer-leader for life. The truer understanding of the love of God and of the reality of life has been seen more in liberation theology and in such areas as Latin America and other parts of the world where poverty, oppression and suffering are known to be realities of life than in the prosperous areas of the Western world.

The love of God has been better understood in Latin America because, as a German theologian has said:

> In Europe, Christmas and Easter are the high points of the church year . . . to Indians and peasants of Chile and Brazil their feast is Holy Week. The suffering and death of Jesus, the pain and mourning, is something in which they can share. There they are at home. That is their life.[5]

In Latin America Mary, the mother of Jesus, is not the bejewelled, gorgeously dressed and painted image of wealth and aristocracy seen in the shrines of Europe, but rather is she the centre of the symbols of liberation. She is the Our Lady of Guadalupe at Tepeyac in Mexico, who has become the patroness of Latin America. Why? Because the vision was given to a poor Indian, Juan Diego, at a time when Indians were persecuted and Indian women raped by Spanish con-querors. Through this vision millions of Indians regained their dignity and desire to live. Now, nearly four hundred and fifty years later, the devotion continues to grow. Through it millions of oppressed people all over that part of the American continent most noted for tyranny, torture, evil rulers and obscene divisions of wealth and poverty, continue to find in her an icon of life, future hope and security. My hope is that this true understanding of Mary as symbol of liberation may replace the thinking of Immaculate Concep-tion (a slur on human sexuality) and Heavenly Assumption (the thinking of rulers and their glory rather than the ruled and their poverty).

Perhaps the reason why the Western world finds the God who enters into, rather than releases from, suffering difficult to cope with is because we try to pretend that there is a gospel for the rich as well as for the poor. But nowhere in the gospels do we find any gospel for the rich, only a gospel which is available to us when we have not allowed our possessions and our greed for wealth to take us over. There are many warnings of the dangers of riches: what shall it profit a man if he gain the whole world and lose his own soul?, the stories of Dives and Lazarus, of the rich young ruler, the rich fool, and so on. There are no beatitudes for riches, rather the reverse. Christ's proclamation of the kingdom of God is quite clear:

> He has sent me to announce good news to the poor, to proclaim release for prisoners and recovery of sight for the blind;
> to let the broken victims go free,
> to proclaim the year of the Lord's favour. (Luke 4: 18–19)

And again in the beatitudes:

> How blessed are you who are in need; the kingdom of God is yours.
> How blessed are you who now go hungry; your hunger shall be satisfied.
> How blessed are you who weep now; you shall laugh . . .
> But alas for you who are rich; you have had your time of happiness.
> Alas for you who are well-fed now; you shall go hungry. (Luke 6: 20–25)

The world would no doubt rewrite the beatitudes somewhat on these lines:

> Blesssed are the rich – for theirs is the kingdom of God.
> Blessed are the strong – for they shall inherit the earth.
> Blessed are the happy – for they shall find life easy.
> Blessed are those who hunger after riches and status – for they shall be filled.
> Blessed are the ruthless – for they shall obtain what they want.

So the first necessity in the church of the future is firmly to proclaim the Gospel, not as a refuge from the insecurities of the world but as identification *with* those insecurities – the Gospel that is firmly on the side of the poor, the oppressed, the blind (blinded by false imagery, prejudice, gut-reactions prompted by corrupted media, etc.) and the enslaved (enslaved by poverty, class, possessions, sex, drugs, drink). Then the church will enable its members, in their search for truth, to live with the insecurity necessary to that search; and in their search for the kingdom of God the church will enable them to identify in sensitivity and action with the insecure, in order to bring nearer their release from the unnecessary insecurities imposed by human beings. When Christ warns against riches he is not giving sanctity to poverty but rather showing that life needs to be balanced. As he says in the beatitudes and in the story of Dives and Lazarus, those who have had their undue share of the world's goods have had their time of happiness – in our parlance they have 'had it'! – they cannot expect more. If they prefer the short-term pleasures of riches on earth, they have made their choice; the warning is that they lose the eternal joys of oneness with God.

I have spent some time on the theology of the God who is identified with the poor and with powerlessness, because I am convinced that the reason the Western churches are despised and neglected is because they have not so identified themselves. The faith which will gain respect in an age like ours is the faith which resists rather than encourages the shallow demands for instant success, instant wealth, instant pleasure. It is the faith which does not look for securities, which is not constantly wanting life to be without pain. The faith needed now is one that knows that the God of the cross does not and – if she is true to her nature – cannot automatically and immediately make all things right. Rather does she 'let be' what goes wrong, suffering and redeeming the consequences in a love that does not let go. So, when everything is going wrong for me, at a profound level in God everything is all right, for everything is the love which is with me, involved with me in the depths. Love does not let go: 'Love is not love which alters when it alteration finds.'

Western society often seems to have a disposable attitude towards human relationships as well as to things: for

94

example, regarding marriage as serial rather than permanent, friends as useful rather than long-standing, and drop-
ping telephone calls and visits when someone has left the
area or been bereaved. There is, of course, a 'letting-go'
which can be a loving and caring action; this is when it is
for a greater reason – as when Christ drew away from his
family or when someone you love finds a deeper relationship
with another. But the God who lets go does so only for
greater love, not for lack of love, and that should be also
true for us.

Jim Cotter in one of his books of prayer puts this well
when he writes:

> Perhaps I do not have the confidence of a previous
> century proclaiming with strong confidence 'Firmly I
> believe and truly', but yet I do have the confidence that
> comes from the inner love of God, the God who is most
> with me when he appears to be absent from me and I
> can whisper if not shout:

> Barely I believe yet truly
> God is One and God is Three
> God is love and seen most fully
> Hanging from the wintry tree.[6]

A LIBERATION THEOLOGY FOR THE FUTURE CHURCH

Having outlined what is meant by a God of love as proclaimed by Christ, what then are the implications of this for
the thinking and teaching of the church in relation to the
poor, the oppressed, the enslaved? Again it is with the reality
of what is, rather than the wishful thinking of what might
be or ought to be, that I shall be concerned.

First, those of us who are Anglicans will need to have a
different image of ourselves as a church. We shall not see
ourselves as the established church, part of the culture of
the nation and therefore needing to avoid being disturbing
to state authority. Instead, we shall see ourselves as a creative

minority in a pluralistic society containing much variety of belief, social attitude and political ideology. The church does not represent a majority, nor has it for some time (if ever), and it is not likely to do so in the future. So it has no need to behave as if it were ever fearful of offending an image of itself as the embodiment of so-called 'English' middle-class values. The way forward for the church is not the way of conformity. Rather it should heed the words of Martin Luther King:

> This hour in history needs a dedicated circle of trans-formed non-conformists ... the saving of our world from pending doom will come not through the com-placent adjustment of the conforming majority but through the creative maladjustment of a non-conform-ing minority.[7]

The words 'the creative maladjustment of a non-conform-ing minority' look very like a description of the prophets of the Old Testament, especially Isaiah, Hosea and Jeremiah. This is exactly what the function of the church should be – a combination of prophetic understanding of what love, justice, freedom and significance mean in terms of the con-text of contemporary society together with a lack of inhi-bition in expressing that understanding and acting upon it. And in order that this understanding may reach all sections of society there has to be a capacity to recognise the different levels of understanding and communication to which the task of education must be adjusted and addressed. At present we are only able to conform to and address limited sections of society. A parish priest has written:

> As the vicar of a struggling outer-estate church, I find that increasingly the structure of a hierarchical middle-class established church is unable to respond to the needs of local people who, it would seem from the gos-pels, should not only be the first recipients of our good news but also the first we listen to. Instead they have been forgotten and ignored. As I struggle to respond to that theological perception I find myself constantly diverted by the demands of my fellow Christians,

whether bishops or local congregation, that have placed conformity, survival, the *status quo*, above the breaking-in of the kingdom of God. Consequently I find myself isolated at times and wonder if I have just misunderstood what the church is about. It is time that alternative voices not only shared their whispers but started proclaiming as well.[8]

This parish priest is right; my own experience would bear out every word he has said. At the level of communication the church fails to interest either the intellectual or the relatively uneducated. The intellectual naturally and rightly scorns the crude fundamentalism which prefers dogmatic absolutism to the free search for truth which relativises all-truth claims. At the other end of the intellectual spectrum, many people within our inner cities and council estates do not understand the language or the liturgies we use, as it is not their normal way of thinking or expressing themselves. Most either have no religion at all or find their 'folk religion', based upon instinct and emotion rather than concepts, written off by so-called 'committed' Christians. The church seems able to communicate only with those who read *The Times*, the *Independent* or the *Telegraph*, not with those who read the *Sun*. This means that large sections of the population are not reached by either our theology or liturgy. Why do the relatively uneducated read the tabloids? Is it because the language and degree of concentration these papers require is within their natural capacity? There is nothing wrong with that; the sadness is that those who know how to use the right language communicate what panders to the lowest of gut-reaction instincts – crude, semi-fascist, sexist and soft-porn material. The tabloids know how to communicate, but they under-estimate and treat with contempt the capacity of their readers to assimilate better ideas. The church needs to be able to communicate the ideas of Hans Küng, Moltmann, Don Cupitt or David Jenkins in the language of the *Sun*. This is a difficult task but it can be done: John Robinson was once asked to set out the main ideas of *Honest to God* in an article in the *Daily Mirror* using their language – which he did very successfully. The task of communication in simple but not simplistic terms is one that should be given more attention by the church.

If then the church is to fulfil its role as a prophetic, creatively maladjusted minority relating, in the words of Moltmann, the text to the context and to be able to do that in the language and understanding of many differing sections of society, it must spend a great deal of its time in *listening*.

Let me for a moment return to two of the models suggested by John Taylor. If we are to fulfil the second model, of being an interpretative fellowship, reflecting on our faith in relation to whatever aspect of the human situation we are confronting, then we have to listen to the actual situation in which people find themselves and therefore to the people who are in that situation.

This may be done in various ways. Sometimes we shall draw people of differing groups, backgrounds and attitudes together, as I did in Camberwell; sometimes we shall draw together people involved in the same situation of work or neighbourhood, as I did in Woldingham. In both cases we shall listen very carefully to not only what is being said, but to what is being felt and what lies beneath what is being said. This listening will be done not only in formal groups, because many people will never come to groups organised by the church.

In every area there are other groups in which people express their needs, grievances and feelings: for example, trade unions, local authority council meetings, tenants' associations and many recreational and social groups, such as pubs, clubs, Women's Institutes, youth associations. Much will be learnt from such non-churchy groups, and in our training of church members, they should be encouraged to join such groups and taught how to listen to what is being said and how to see what is being said in the context of the Gospel. There will be a need not only to listen to *what* is being said but also to *how* it is being said – what language is used, what images of communication, what personal experience, what is being revealed of background and gut-reactions.

In the third of John Taylor's models, that of being a

dynamically responsible fellowship enabling its members to rise to their full human potential and thereby promoting necessary change, it will be necessary both to know what is preventing people, inside and outside the church, from rising to their full human potential and what are the changes needed within the situation being considered. What, for example, is preventing the poor and the rich from rising to their full human potential? Moltmann identifies these impediments to fulfilment:

> The poor are all those who have to endure acts of violence and injustice without being able to defend themselves. The poor are all who have to exist physically and spiritually on the fringe of death, who have nothing to live for and to whom life has nothing to offer. The poor are all who are at the mercy of others, and who live with empty and open hands. Poverty therefore means both dependency and openness ... It is an expression which describes the enslavement and dehumanisation of man in more than one dimension.

And what does he say about the rich?

> The opposite of the poor in the Old Testament is the man of violence who oppresses the poor, forces them into poverty and enriches himself at their expense. 'Riches' are equally multi-dimensional and extend from economic exploitation, by way of social supremacy, to the complacency of the people who look after themselves in every sector of life, ignore the rights of others and do not want to have to say 'thank-you' to anyone for anything ... The rich are all the people who live with tightly clenched hands. They are neither dependent on others nor open for others. The rich will only be helped when they recognise their own poverty and enter the fellowship of the poor.[9]

There is, therefore, a twofold poverty which Christ recognised, and it is a poverty which spans the centuries and is still with us today. The poverty of the poor is their powerlessness, dependence and lack of significance and stature within our society. In England that is seen at its worst among the ethnic

minorities, especially among the West Indians and Paki-
stanis, and in the increasing divisions between the very rich
and the very poor. The poverty of the rich is their absorption
with themselves, their reliance on their riches and their lack
of a sense of sharing with and responsibility for the poor.
This has been seen most forcibly in the lack of sensitivity
which enables already rich directors of banks and other
financial institutions to see no illogicality in stressing the
need for wage restraint, while at the same time allowing
themselves to take huge increases in salary far above the
rate of inflation.

I said earlier that there is no gospel for the rich, but I
should, perhaps, have qualified that by saying that there is
no gospel for the rich in their riches, but there *is* a 'good
news' which applies to them as well as to the poor; both
gospels are concerned with the importance of what is real
being, and freedom from false being. The good news which
Christ is wanting to bring is good news to both the poor
and the rich: good news for the poor in giving them that
sense of worth which the fight against their poverty will
bring to them, so that powerlessness becomes in a true
sense power; good news to the rich in freeing them, by the
reduction of their riches, from that servitude to possessions
which is truly crippling to the spirit and by which they are
able to feel a wholly false sense of power and superiority,
which makes them oppressive to the poor. It is a mistake to
think that Christ is against the rich man and for the poor
man as such; he is against the accumulation of riches and
the impoverishment of poverty for the same reason – that
both tend to destroy the essential eternal being of a person
as made in the image of God. Schumacher puts this well
when he says:

> Our ordinary mind always tries to persuade us that we
> are nothing but acorns and that our greatest happiness
> is to become bigger, fatter, shinier acorns; but that is of
> interest only to pigs. Our faith gives us knowledge
> of something much better: that we can become oak
> trees.[10]

Schumacher maintains that we each choose our grade of

being – what he calls our grade of significance – but if we choose a lower grade than we need then not only our whole life suffers but the world in which we live and our relations to other people suffer too. The church's task is to enable both rich and poor to have the highest possible grade of being. The poor are diminished by their poverty, so for them the need is for the church to align itself with their struggle against degrading poverty. The rich are also being diminished by their riches, as, for example, when in an age of recession and fight against the evils of inflation their greed takes precedence over sharing in wage restraint. According to Schumacher, it is only when my life is geared to the higher levels, to love of God or to levels of being above my own that I am able to love my neighbour:

> ... the 'higher' the person, the greater and richer is his or her world. A person, for instance, entirely fixed in the philosophy of materialistic scientism, denying the reality of the 'invisibles' and confining his attention solely to what can be counted, measured and weighed, lives in a very poor world [in which] only a very impoverished kind of life can be lived. The universe is what it is; but he who, although *capax universi*, limits himself to its lowest sides – to his biological needs, his creature comforts or his accidental encounters – will inevitably 'attract' a miserable life ... The higher the level of being, the greater, richer and more wonderful is the world.[11]

The proclamation of the Gospel needs then to take a completely different form. At present we see poor people as objects of compassion and solicitude but we do not usually see rich people in that way. As a result our attitude to each is very different, and throughout the history of the churches there has been a strange ambivalence. On the one hand the church has not been lacking in care and concern for the poor: as seen in the works of many monastic orders of both past and present, and of individuals, in the inner cities and in poverty-stricken country areas; on the other hand, the church never seemed to be able to avoid that 'kow-towing' to the rich so denounced by St James but so widely practised. The rich, despite the many warnings of the Gospel, have been looked upon as the fortunate whose responsibility was to be 'do-gooders' to the poor. Too often the result has been a patronising sympathy from above for the poor and unconscious identification with the rich, whom the church placates in order to gain their support.

To sum up this section about what I mean by a thinking church and by theology relating to life in accordance with the criteria of reality and creativity, I see need for three changes to come about:

1. A recognition that reality requires us not to expect unending happiness as a natural right, but rather to accept the daily insecurities of life. The task of the church then is to provide, not escapes from or answers to these insecurities, but rather the identification and sharing of a God of love – to be there with people when needed. The Gospel does not give us security but enables us to live with insecurity.

2. A realisation that, similarly in our search for truth, there are no true-for-all-time orthodoxies but rather, in each generation, further insights into the truth of God, of life and the meaning and purpose of our existence.

We have built up in the course of centuries complicated systems of orthodoxy, some of which, such as the Nicene Creed, we repeat every Sunday in our worship. Within the various groupings of Christianity there have been heated arguments as to who is right and even wars and persecutions as people have been tortured and burnt for what is called heresy. But who are these heretics? Simply those who have found themselves at variance with majority opinion at any particular time; later it may be that their heresies are accepted! The other fault in the assessment of what is called heresy is that it is always measured by a certain period in the past rather than by the needs of the word of Christ in the present, and the selection of those periods is itself arbitrary.

I hope, therefore, that the church of the future will

neither descend to a fundamentalist literalism which no one of intelligence could be expected to accept, nor to a rigid traditionalism demanding adherence to fixed formulae and the calling of all those who do not accept such formulae as heretics. I hope too that the future church will never abandon that searching spirit, characteristic of the 1960s, in which 'truth is not the position you hold but the path you tread, a path without a destination and whose course is unpredictable'.[12] Let the assessments of truth be: is this view of humanity, of life, of God, according to boundaries of reality, the needs of love, the fulfilment of creativity? That would seem to be as good a test as any of whether or not we are treading on the path of truth.

3. It will be by this testing that the church will do its work of thinking and action: namely, the testing of the real, the loving and the creative in all fields of life. This will be done at various levels: those of us who are theologians in the way we talk about God, humanity, the meaning and goals of life both immanent and transcendent, and about the ethics of sex, ecology, work, peace, national and international politics; those of us who are communicators in the language and imagery we use to reach all levels of understanding and education, both in our worship and our writings; those of us who are activists in seeking to change that area of the world's life for which, under God, we take responsibility – to meet the real needs of both rich and poor, to free the oppressed, the blind and the enslaved. We shall realise then that it is we, not God, who have to do things about poverty in our own country and in the Third World, about famine and starvation, about homelessness, the environment, peace and war, corruption, tyranny and injustice. As far as we can see, God works now only through human beings. If we do not show realism, love and creativity in what we do with our world, then it will steadily go on becoming more and more destructive and death-dealing; no magical action by some being from outside will change things. God works through us and through us alone – we are his incarnations, and this is how it should be. This is the meaning of the

incarnation of Christ. This is the meaning of human beings made in the image of God.

In the light of all that I have said about the thinking church of the future, I shall in the following chapters move into certain specific areas and see what thinking and action based upon realism, love and creativity could and should mean in the future.

1 Dietrich Bonhoeffer, *Ethics* (Fontana 1964), pp. 228, 230.
2 Kenneth Leech, *Spirituality and Pastoral Care* (Sheldon Press 1986), pp. 33, 136.
3 Dietrich Bonhoeffer, *Letters and Papers from Prison* (enlarged edn SCM Press 1971), p. 360f., as quoted in Moltmann's *The Crucified God.*
4 Jurgen Moltmann, *The Crucified God* (SCM Press 1974), p. 243.
5 H. Lüning, quoted by Moltmann in *The Crucified God.*
6 Jim Cotter, *Prayers for a Time of Healing* (privately published).
7 Martin Luther King, *Strength to Love* (Fontana 1969), pp. 23–4.
8 In *Trust* (newsletter of the SCM Press), no. 3, April 1991.
9 Jurgen Moltmann, *The Church in the Power of the Spirit* (SCM Press 1977), p. 79.
10 E. F. Schumacher, *A Guide for the Perplexed* (Jonathan Cape 1977), p. 149.
11 Ibid., pp. 45–6.
12 Don Cupitt, *Radicals and the Future of the Church* (SCM Press 1989), p. 60.

17

A SEXUAL ETHIC FOR THE FUTURE

I have already shown, in chapter 10, some of the ways in which the thinking and action of the church are unrealistic in the area of sexuality. In 1977 a positive step forward was taken by the Anglican Church when a resolution was passed in the General Synod by a large majority in the following terms:

> This Synod:
> 1. Feels that the time has come for a new look at the whole Christian theology of sexuality in the light of present theological and psychiatric understanding.
> 2. Calls upon the Board for Social Responsibility to make a preliminary study of the principal issues involved for debate.

I proposed this resolution but, despite the massive support it gained, that study was never done and the whole resolution was brushed aside after a two-hour discussion at the following synod at York. Subsequent debates in recent years, notably the Higton debate, have shown all the failings and prejudices outlined in the background I have given. In the Higton debate no attention was given to the complicated issues involved in concern for fulfilling and creative human relationships: instead, as has so often been the case through centuries, the whole debate fastened its attention on genital sexual activity – what happens below the belt rather than the above-the-belt complex of body/mind/spirit unity of human love in all its forms.

Recently, however, a registered charity has been formed

to deal with this lack of understanding in the church about sexuality. It is the Institute for the Study of Christianity and Sexuality (I.S.C.S.). By study days, conferences, seminars, workshops and publications, I.S.C.S. provides a forum for the development of a comprehensive and positive theology and spirituality in all areas of human sexuality and relationship. Some of the conferences and study days held have been on such subjects as 'Christianity and Sexuality', 'Power and Moral Authority', 'Monogamy', 'Celibacy', 'Distorted Images: a study of pornography and theology of desire'.* This is exactly the kind of serious, positive and objective study the church needs.

Most of our difficulties within the church seem to have arisen from following, and distorting, the Pauline view of the division of flesh and spirit, and from allowing ourselves to be guided by out-dated cultures of a previous age. Gender-identity and sexual-identity in human beings are very largely the creation of culture. Much of our sexual ethic derives from a culture which saw men and women in a very different way from today, but in the church we are still very much in the male-dominated society of the ancient Jewish world.

We need a more Johannine theology of the wholeness and unity of flesh and spirit as the basis for dealing with the personal problems which confront people today, and we need to adopt the attitude of 'in Christ there is no male nor female' to guide our considerations of gender and sexuality. If we start with the definition of sexuality as a gift, an experience, a creative energy, a joy – the consummation of relational fulfilment – then we are in line with the whole gospel of God in creation, the understanding of humans as made in the image of God, and the fulfilment of that image in Jesus who affirms in body as well as in mind and spirit that God is love. A true understanding of the Scriptures starts from these positive affirmations rather than by searching for 'proof' texts which are more related to a previous culture than to our belief in God as creator and redeemer of all that we are.

* Details of the future programme of I.S.C.S. and a placing on the mailing list can be obtained from I.S.C.S., Oxford House, Derbyshire Street, London E2 6HG. Tel. 071-731 1249.

I would offer the following five guidelines for a theology of wholeness and realistic affirmation in accordance with the mind and understanding of Christ: (1) all relationships in life are intended to be creative; (2) accept people (including oneself) as they are and the situation as it is, and then act in the way that is best in that situation; (3) seek to follow the pattern of being and creativity given us by God in the life of Jesus; (4) recognise that sexuality may rightly be expressed in varying ways and that emphasis in sexuality has moved from the biological urge for procreation to the personal expression of love; and (5) recognise the liberation from sexism and male domination shown by Christ and give more value to feminine attributes. In the following pages I shall develop these guidelines more fully.

1. All human beings are made in the image of God, which means that all relationships of life are meant to be creative and not destructive. This means that in our sexual activities with another – whether of different sex or same sex – there is no room for exploitation or possessiveness. Nor can sexuality be separated from the rest of personality, because such sexual encounters would be diminishing to the individual and thereby uncreative and destructive. In sexuality as in the rest of life the definition of love given by Solovyev holds true: 'The meaning and worth of love consists in this, that it effectually constrains us to acknowledge for another the unconditional significance of which we are conscious in ourselves.'[1]

Objection by Christians to pornography and page 3 of the *Sun* are not based upon moral prudery but upon the degradation of the flesh and the diminishment of women. The Christian who is concerned with the mind of Christ would, however, equally reject the subjugation of the female and the inequality of the human image represented in the words of St Paul: 'While every man has Christ for his Head, woman's head is man, as Christ's Head is God ... man is the image of God and the mirror of his glory, whereas woman reflects the glory of man' (1 Corinthians 11:3, 7). If that were true it is very strange that in our society the rate of crime and violence is far greater amongst men than women and the worst excesses of brutality, sex and murder are usually by men – the 'mirror of God's glory'!

2. Study of humanity shows that, while we are made in the image of God, we are also always becoming what we are meant to be. The myth of the Fall indicates that human relationships are marred by three factors: the desire to have everything easy and instant ('Ye shall be as gods'); the failure to be open to each other and the desire to cover up (the fig leaves); and the abdication of responsibility and the wish to blame others (the man blamed the woman, the woman blamed the snake).

All these factors are obvious in human relationships, sexual as well as other relationships – promiscuity, guilt and lack of trust, irresponsibility and desire to project on to others our own guilts. So we cannot expect sexual relationships any more than any other relationships of life to be unmarred by human frailty. (When I hear of the 'exposures' in which some of the tabloid newspapers delight, I wonder if the editors' own lives are so pure as, from their shock at human frailty, they apparently would like others to think. Sometimes the more mischievous part of myself would like to find some disgraceful scandal in the lives of those editors who so lightly humiliate and destroy the reputation of those who are simply sinners like themselves!)

Moreover, we have to remember, in a more realistic ethic, that we all inherit a past which influences and conditions us and that we live in a present which is in many ways unalterable. Therefore all life and all morality are inevitably situational. The circumstances of the situation limit the possibilities of action. A marriage which has gone dead has gone dead – it cannot be dealt with as if it were alive. A pregnancy conceived irresponsibly has happened – it is of little help to say that it should not have happened. A disease born of promiscuity is now a sickness – condemnation and imposition of guilt will not help. A homosexual is a homosexual, and so should not be treated as if he or she could be a heterosexual just by choosing to be. So in every case what has to be done will be the best possible within the *given* situation, not in some non-realistic ideal situation.

3. God has given us the pattern of our true being and creativity in the life and humanity of Jesus. According to St Paul (Ephesians 4:13) the motivation of life is to come to 'mature manhood, measured by nothing less than the full stature of Christ'. Unfortunately the mature manhood of Jesus gives little help to the understanding of our sexuality, since the gospels contain no recorded evidence of the way in which Jesus dealt with his sexuality. This, of course, is not surprising, since none of the earlier gospel writers were concerned with the personal life of Jesus in that sense. They were not writing a biography. They were writing to convert people by the Good News of Jesus as the incarnation of a God of love, redeeming us through reconciliation, forgiveness, healing and, above all, life through death. The early church, unlike readers of the tabloids, would not have been the slightest bit interested in details of the love-life of Jesus! On the other hand, if Jesus was to be the pattern of true humanity he could not have been asexual. The church does no service to him or to ourselves by pretending that Jesus had no sexual feelings or attractions, since if that were so he would have been no true human being.

The only slight evidence we have is that there were degrees of closeness and intimacy in the relationship of Jesus with those who were his constant associates: the disciples Peter, James and John were always chosen for the important occasions when he wanted support and help. If the witness of John himself is to be believed, he himself was the closest of all – 'the disciple whom Jesus loved'. Nor was there any disassociation from physical nearness in their intimacy: for example, John was 'leaning on Jesus' bosom' at the Last Supper. Mary Magdalene also seems to have had a special place; she alone was chosen to be the first witness of the resurrection. Why? Do we not usually in times of crisis want to reassure those who have been closest to us? Were the words, 'Do not touch me', perhaps addressed to one who was accustomed to give affectionate embraces to him? Maybe

Jesus, in choosing as his closest in affection a man and a woman, is indicating to us that 'mature manhood' means that in Christ there is no male or female in separate stereotype, but that we are capable, without guilt, of recognising and accepting the male and female within each of us and our attraction to both.

4. An affirmative and realistic view of sexuality would also mean recognition that the ways in which human embodiment is expressed in behaviour are many and various. We often speak of a child's need to learn the 'facts of life', but what are the facts of life in the complex areas of human sexuality? How do we arrive at a definition of what is normal and what is deviant? It has been said that there is no form of sexual activity that is not deviant at some time in some social location or with some partners in some specified relationships.

What are the criteria of what is correct sexual activity and what is not? What are the criteria of what is wholeness and what is disability or sickness? How do we determine what actions are criminal, what constitutes evil or sin? Why do some cultures tolerate, and regard as normal, behaviour which in other cultures is regarded as 'not natural'. I would mention just two factors which are obvious in the study of sexual embodiment and gender:

(a) Despite the constant assertion that procreation is the only justifiable use of human sexual activity, the reality of sexuality is that often its expression has little to do with procreation, and the pleasures and drives of sexual expression go far beyond the needs of biological procreation.

Freud's thinking revolutionised many ideas about human nature and its sexual expression. He drew attention to a dimension of childhood sensual gratification which has an enduring effect upon our lives. The young child is a mass of instinctual needs which pass through the sequences of oral, anal and phallic. Freud demonstrated that the child first experiences sensual satisfaction through the mouth, then the anus with its smooth membrane providing physical pleasure, and finally the focus turns to the phallic. These are certainly statements of fact, whatever the truth of his theories, and it is equally a fact that, whatever morality may say about there being only one way of natural human intercourse, many human beings have found bodily pleasure without guilt in the oral and anal parts of the body as means of satisfaction and fulfilment, even fulfilment of feelings of strong affection and love. If the general attitude to sexuality has changed, as Dominian says,[2] from the biological to the personal – where pleasure and love often lead naturally to sexual expression – then it is no use condemning certain forms of sexual activity simply because they do not lead to procreation or because they conflict with our preconceived ideas about what is appropriate and what is not.

(b) Sexual gender is also a complex matter in the assessment of reality. In the human development of most people sexual differentiation follows a consistent pattern – either male or female – but in a minority there may be sexual ambiguity at one or more levels. Sometimes a sex chromosome is omitted or duplicated, leading to sexual immaturity, sterility or inappropriate bodily shape. Occasionally there is someone who is not clearly male or female, to the extent that a sexual change is not only possible but accords with reality.

Gender identity is also not necessarily straightforward. A man may possess what, in our culture, are usually called feminine characteristics; he is often disparagingly called 'effeminate'. Or a woman may possess those characteristics of the male which are equally scorned as 'butch'. But it is well to realise that attitudes to these characteristics are often determined by cultural or ethnic ideas rather than based on facts. Both gender and sexual identity may be a creation of culture and have nothing to do with morality or with religious thinking. For example, if it is generally agreed that kissing is an expression of love, on what grounds is kissing to be denied if it is between two males, and in England even made a criminal offence if it is in public? Is love between males morally wrong or is such condemnation simply expression of a 'macho' view of appropriate male behaviour, which again varies from country to country? In English culture, for example, any display of emotion between two males, whether of affection or of sorrow, is viewed with distaste; in many Mediterranean and Latin cultures men will hold hands, embrace, kiss and weep publicly without rousing any suspicion of abnormal behaviour.

Amidst then all the many variations of sexuality which we find in fact, it is increasingly difficult to have rigid and dogmatic views of what is right or wrong when viewed as a matter of realism. A truly Christian point of view will see right and wrong in sexual behaviour not from preconceived moral attitudes dating from different cultures of the past but from what is most truly creative and fulfilling to the individual within the circumstances of the given personal situation.

5. The final affirmative guideline is the liberation which Christ gives us from sexism and male dominance. This is particularly needed in the church, for perhaps nowhere in society is the placid assumption of male dominance so strong as in the ordering of the church. It is this male dominance syndrome which lies behind many of the respectable arguments put forward against the ordination of women. As I have already said, St Paul all too readily took for granted the headship of men over women, presumably on the basis of the words to Eve in Genesis 3:16: 'Your yearning shall be for your husband, yet he will lord it over you.'

However, it seems that Paul forgot that this domination came as the result of sin; when the mythic fruit is eaten man tries to be not only made in the image of God, but one with God by a short cut. Thus the perfect equality of male and female in humankind is broken and disorder enters into all human relationships, with God and with each other: nakedness now creates shame; what was united is now divided; and what was equal is now to be unequal – man is to dominate over woman. This lording-it model is one from which society is only slowly liberating itself, and even now it is still the cause of the stupid 'macho' image which perpetuates, often through the media, that idea of the aggressive male attitude to sex which lies behind rape and violence.

112

We should long ago have recognised that this model is one of disorder as a result of sin, not a model of the ordering of God.

Unfortunately, however, the dominance of man over woman has come to be thought of in our liturgy and in our church structures as if it were the model of God: in the marriage service the woman has been handed over by one male, her father, to another male, her husband; the model of family life has been the man as the head and the woman as the obedient servant of the family (the model of Proverbs 31); and in the Catholic, Orthodox and, until very recently, most Protestant churches all the authority and decisions have been with the male – the woman has been allotted the 'kitchen' jobs of the church. This model, as Don Cupitt points out, has become the philosophic as well as the structural model of religion. Form and order belong to the male and, therefore, to God as the male God; change and impurity belong to the female who has, therefore, to be ritually purified:

> The connexion between God, masculinity, form and the rational soul, on the one hand, and between woman, matter and corruptibility on the other was built into philosophy, science and theology at their inception . . . so man's domination of woman provided the basic pattern in which thought operated . . . God as the male of males, lordly, active and creative, spiritual and supreme in perfection, power and wisdom.[3]

So, in the future of the church, we need to change both our image of God and of the male: to see instead the weakness of God as her strength and greatest help to suffering humanity; the Christ in whom there is neither male nor female; men and women possessing, in varying degrees, wisdom, strength, sensitivity and love; and everyone used in the structure of the church not according to stereotyped images but according to their individual abilities and gifts. The ordination of women is a good way to start showing that the maleness of Christ is in reality an accident of culture rather than a divinely pre-ordained ruling.

These, then, are the guidelines which I hope could lead to a future church more positive, realistic and creative in its attitude to all aspects of human sexuality.

There are, of course, other areas linked with sexuality, such as abortion, artificial insemination and embryo research, which require more detailed consideration than I can give. These are dealt with by the Institute for the Study of Christianity and Sexuality, and if the church could be seen to take a lead in supporting the work of I.S.C.S. – and in promoting a realistic and creative attitude towards all issues of sexuality – it would be educating its own members away from moral dogmatism and self-righteousness towards learning rather more of the mind of Christ. It would also be helping to move the media away from fantasy to reality in its dealings with sexual morality and thus educating the images and stereotypes held in society. Changes of attitude by the church could help society to rethink its present oppressive and often cruel persecutions of those who do not fit into the sexual 'norms'. Too often, at present, the churches seem to collude with, rather than to correct, the oppressive sexism of society, but such is not the task of a church whose function is to

> stand over against its surroundings, culture and environment and see God revealed in weakness and God-forsakenness, in darkness and negation. The theology of the cross is a theology of contradiction, of protest, of conflict, a theology which refuses an easy conformity with conventional norms and attitudes.[4]

1 V. Solovyev, *The Meaning of Love* (trans. J. Marshall, G. Bles 1945), p. 59.
2 Jack Dominian, *Proposals for a New Sexual Ethic*, Darton, Longman and Todd 1977.
3 Don Cupitt, *Radicals and the Future of the Church* (SCM Press 1989), pp. 45, 46.
4 Kenneth Leech, *True God* (Sheldon Press 1985), pp. 313–14.

114

18

MARRIAGE AND REMARRIAGE
IN A FUTURE CHURCH

For years the church has been wrestling with the problem of how, when it believes in the indissolubility of marriage, it can best help people whose marriage has come apart to make another relationship of marriage and have it blessed by the church. But underlying this problem there is another. Is marriage simply a secular reality and contract which can be broken if situations change or is marriage a sacramental reality of creation which cannot be broken? ('Those whom God has joined together let no man put asunder.')

REALITIES OF MARRIAGE

In attempting to apply the criteria of reality and creativity to the vexed questions of marriage and divorce, we have to take into account the following facts which cannot be gainsaid simply by applying a rigid doctrine of indissolubility:

1. How do we know that every couple who stand at the altar rail and are joined in legal marriage have been joined together by God? May not they themselves, in believing this, have made a mistake which later shows? Couples come together for marriage for such mixed reasons – sexual attraction, family pressure, social and financial need – that it would be very rash to assume that, just because some words are said in a church, this means that God has joined them. I have known many occasions when family and friends said,

what later became apparent, that the couple should never have married; they were incompatible. It may well have been that God was on the same side as those parents and friends, but God no more overrules our mistakes than he does our sins!

2. It is quite clear that biblical views of marriage are based upon belief and relationship to God. Schillebeeckx makes this point strongly in his valuable study of marriage, *Marriage – Human Reality and Saving Mystery*, where he maintains that the indissolubility of marriage is based upon the human essence of marriage itself as called into existence by the Creator (and, therefore, part of the whole act of creation as an underlying unity of all things*); the basis of absolute indissolubility is to be found in Christian baptism and so 'the will of the Creator', to which Christ referred, means that marriage as a human reality is a reality that includes a religious relationship with God – the saving relationship that was concretely provided in Christ – and thus formally falls to the share of man by faith and baptism.[1] Schillebeeckx regards the sacramental presence of Christ at the marriage as a means by which a secular reality becomes a sacrament and so calls the couple to a higher sacramental bonding than the natural:

> Christ is present when the marriage is contracted and he is there in order to do and say something ... Christ himself wishes to give these two to each other for life, so that their human love may be able to rise above its natural limitations and become a sacred sign of a greater and deeper love – a love like that which he himself has for his people – the church.[2]

But again the reality is often very different in the secular situation of today. My experience over many years is that most of the couples I have married have only a very rudimentary understanding of the Christian faith, and certainly do

---

*It could be said that the indissolubility of marriage and ecological respect for the environment have the same theological background – the unity and interdependence of all in creation with God.

116

not see themselves as partaking in any sacramental relationship to be likened to the unity of Christ with his church, despite the fact that these words are in the marriage service.

3. Other realities which work against lifelong commitment are:

(a) The intrusion of 'romantic love' as a basis for marriage. 'Falling in love' has very little to do with stability or permanence in marriage, since 'falling out of love' can be equally as common. Nor is sexual attraction any contribution to marriage commitment – in fact rather the reverse, since if that is a strong feature in the relationship then other more attractive and younger partners will be sought as age diminishes such attraction.

(b) The increasing longevity of life means that far greater testing will be put on the permanence of marriages; what in former times was often a commitment for only about twenty-five years may now become a commitment for fifty or even sixty years.

(c) The general ethos of disposability intrudes also into relationships with people, so that in some sections of society serial marriage has become almost a norm.

(d) There are also more pressures on marriage. Greater equality between the sexes means that women now expect more of marriage than being an obedient housewife and a passive sexual partner. In view of these pressures much more hard work will be necessary to keep two people joined in marriage.

(e) Finally, the hard fact remains that, for whatever reasons, marriages do break down; love dies and therefore, even without divorce, there is no longer the 'one-fleshness' of which the Bible speaks. Are these couples who have failed to maintain indissolubility to be treated as though this is one area in life in which no mistakes can be made, and be condemned to celibacy for the rest of their lives, although this is neither their vocation nor desire? Or are they to persist in a loveless and dead marriage preserving an outward shell from which any true togetherness has departed?

TOWARDS A MORE POSITIVE VIEW OF
MARRIAGE AND REMARRIAGE

1. First there must be a far more thorough consideration of whether or not a marriage is one intended by God by discussing with the couple, well before the marriage, the basic qualities and needs within a relationship which alone will bring lasting commitment. At present the church makes a great deal of fuss about whether to remarry divorced people, but often there is very little put into preparation of those who come to be married.

In one of my parishes where there were many weddings we had a period of training over about three to four months in which all couples were expected to participate. This training was done by married couples who dealt with such matters as: the structure of a marriage – who is going to do what in the areas of finance, housekeeping, child responsibility, etc.; the sexuality of marriage – sensitivity to each other, difficulties which may arise; the bringing up of children; and relationships with the larger community of relatives and friends within which marriage takes place. Only after all that did the clergy come in with the meaning of marriage in sacramental terms and the final rehearsal of the service and its character and meaning. I cannot say whether what we did contributed to the lasting relationship of those we married, but we did, at least, enable each couple to look hard at all that was involved if their marriage was to be successful.

I am sad to see how many churches simply take the necessary details for banns and the marriage service, perhaps have one rehearsal and that is all. How can we expect others to take marriage seriously if we within the church do not take it seriously? I always count it as one of the successes of our pre-marriage training that at least two couples who had this fairly thorough preparation decided after much thought that they should not yet be married.

2. Secondly, just as the preparation for marriage is based upon a serious attempt to discover whether the particular coupling is a true joining by God, so when a marriage has

118

broken down similar testing could be applied to the marriage which has failed before a second relationship is entered upon. Was it ever a true marriage as intended by God, or was it – although not understood at the time – a tragic mistake in that there were from the beginning elements in the relationship and the character of the couple, or at least one of the couple, which rendered the whole marriage null and void – no true marriage?

I have never understood why the doctrine of nullity* practised with considerable thoroughness in the Roman Catholic Church should be so scorned by other churches. I would think that it is more than likely that, if a marriage fails, the causes of that failure were there all the time or, if not there from the beginning, yet became sufficiently clear later for it to be seen that the marriage was no true marriage. The tests applied to nullity in the Roman Catholic Church are very realistic: namely, the intention of permanence, exclusiveness, and possibility of procreation. As these are considered as essentials of marriage and any partner who has an intention against any one of these – that is, against indissolubility, fidelity or having children – is considered to have made the marriage void. Other factors considered include: undue pressure from outside the marriage, incapacity to procreate through impotence or homosexuality, ignorance of the true meaning of marriage, immaturity or a complete change of character in one or both partners so as to make him or her in quality a 'different person'. I would have thought that any one of these circumstances would have made the original marriage no true marriage in the sight of God.

* The advantages of nullity are that it overcomes the undoubted theological difficulty of trying to incorporate the idea that there can be two marriages valid in the sight of God when there can be no question but that biblical evidence supports the possibility of only one. It also takes the whole meaning of marriage and the qualifications for marriage very seriously. If it be argued, as it sometimes is, that it is very difficult to prove that the defects were there from the beginning and that nullity is sometimes abused in favour of the rich and powerful, one could argue that it is equally difficult to prove when a marriage has broken down simply through irresponsibility and lack of work put into the marriage; divorce can also be abused in favour of money or influence!

119

3. There needs also to be a more realistic understanding of human relationships, a recognition that, however much we prepare as thoroughly as we can for marriage within the church, it is unrealistic to expect in a society as secular as ours that people who come to a church for marriage (possibly with an eye more to the setting than to the meaning) will all have that theological and sacramental understanding of divine creation which lies behind the indissolubility of marriage. There are many differing views and grades of commitment.

Even from the earliest days a distinction was made between the marriage of baptised Christians and the marriage of Christians with unbelievers. The absolute indissolubility of marriage was applied only to Christian marriage, and Paul makes this quite clear. Now in a secular society part of our confusion regarding marriage is that many who are, in fact, unbelievers are by social custom married in church, so that the distinction between believer and unbeliever is difficult to discover. Moreover, different degrees of commitment are shown in the increasing tendency for couples to decide to live together, often with complete fidelity to each other but without any official marriage vows. Ironically, it is often when, after several years of such uncommitted living together, the decision is taken to make an official exchange of vows that the partnership breaks down and divorce ensues – perhaps because obligation hinders rather than helps!

If then we are prepared to recognise differing attitudes and standards there are two possibilities:

(a) We can recognise that there is a difference between a secular and a sacramental mystery and that it is not the business of the church to provide a social setting for the non-believer. We can then support the introduction of universal civil marriage for all, as is common in many countries in Europe, followed by the sacrament of marriage in church only for those who accept and understand Christian beliefs. A clear distinction would then be made between what Schillebeeckx calls 'a secular contract and a saving mystery'. This would affect also future action if the marriage should break down; it would be easier for the church to recognise the dissolving of a secular contract, which taken by the state could be dissolved by the state, than the annulling of a sacramental mystery where vows taken within the church could only be annulled, like monastic vows, by the church.

(b) The second possibility is to recognise the differing commitment of a living-together without the permanent commitment of marriage. After all, most of us could not possibly know what it is like to live fully with someone else until we have done so, and there is much to be said for a couple testing this out before taking on the extra responsibility of children; any commitment must be made in the faith that the future alone will prove the truth of what we are doing. Why should it be expected that we can make life-long commitments on the basis of, in many cases, only a few months' or perhaps a year's knowledge of each other, and such knowledge only at the times we meet? Bishop Spong suggests:

> The revival of the institution of betrothal as a recognised relationship, committed and responsible but not legally binding, would in fact help to order and make holy the world of sexual and other testing that now marks the lives of so many young adults.[3]

4. Finally, there is the need to correct many of the assumptions of modern society, and who better than the church for such a work of education? The following are areas where much education needs to be done:

(a) Our culture, through its plays, novels, songs and the media, lays too much emphasis on romantic love as the basis for marriage and the breakdown of relationships. Such a concept of love is a very poor basis for marriage, or indeed for any human relationship; romantic love lays emphasis on feelings, but feelings can change, and often do change, from person to person at different times in life. The love which is likely to be enduring is that which is based upon mutual compatibility and understanding of the sharing of life, not upon some chemistry of attraction, usually sexual. The old semi-arranged marriage according to the needs and compatibilities of the persons concerned was not necessarily a

121

bad contribution to enduring marriage. When my uncle, who was a farmer, was thinking of marriage his family had much discussion with him as to which of the girls in the area, by virtue of their understanding and experience of farming life, would make a good farmer's wife, and his choice had to lie within those limitations. This was also true for most young farmers in the area, and in general these marriages, semi-arranged by the family, worked out very well.

(b) 'One fleshness' means not only the biological joining of male and female but the joining of the male and female within all of us. The old stereotypes of the male as the head, the breadwinner and the 'macho' leader, and the female as the accepting, passive and relatively obedient partner no longer fit in present society. In fact, the old idea of fixed roles for the male and the female has often contributed to the breakdown of a marriage. The questions which need to be raised, and which could form the valuable basis of much discussion within the average parish, are: What are the differences and similarities which separate the sexes and how have these realities been affected for better or worse by the stereotypes within our society and its cultures? Do the models of masculinity or femininity which we have inherited threaten or confirm the sexual identity of both partners? Don Cupitt brings this point out very vividly:

> To this day even in Western countries it is still felt to be appropriate for a woman to be physically smaller and younger than her husband, so that she shall be treated with just a little (but a little is enough in these matters) of teasing and humouring, as if she were a child, a pet or a plaything.[4]

How do I use the feminine traits in me if I am male, or my masculine traits if I am female? The tensions of this male/female polarity will have to be recognised and accepted if human relationships are to work.

(c) Questions of love and hate will also have to be faced. What help, as a church which claims to believe in love, are we giving people to deal with these strong emotions? How do I express anger without causing disruption? Dr Tony

Gough, a pastoral consultant and counsellor, argues that the stresses of a pseudo-peace, a pretending there is no conflict or avoiding conflict, only produces and increases tension in human relationships. He says that what is needed in marriage is to argue creatively, confronting the problems created by our differing attitudes, expressing honestly how we feel and listening to how the other feels; then in the light of that honesty looking jointly at the problem.[5]

There is probably much to be said for this method, but Christians have always found it very difficult to deal with anger and conflict. The attitude of pseudo-peace, often fostered by the church, is a parody of Christian love and much more likely to be destructive in human relationships than constructive, because again it is dealing with pretence rather than with reality.

1 Edward Schillebeeckx, *Marriage – Human Reality and Saving Mystery* (Sheed and Ward 1965), pp. 144 and 159.
2 Ibid., p. xxix.
3 Bishop Spong, *Living in Sin*, Harper and Row, San Francisco, 1988.
4 Don Cupitt, *Radicals and the Future of the Church* (SCM Press 1989), p. 92.
5 Tony Gough, *Couples Arguing*, Darton, Longman and Todd 1987.

19

TOWARDS A CREATIVE VIEW
OF HOMOSEXUALITY

In chapter 10 I wrote of the ignorance of society, and of the church, in current attitudes and dealings with homosexuals. Here I wish to suggest a more creative attitude which I hope the future church will adopt, and which would then reflect itself in society as a whole, including the homosexual minority. There are four steps to be taken: (1) to accept the reality of homosexuality; (2) to enable homosexuals to achieve personal fulfilment within the limitations of their condition; (3) to apply the same ethical criteria to homosexual relationships as to other relationships; and (4) for homosexuals to see how their limitations may be transcended.

1. First it will be necessary to take a realistic look at what is meant by the term 'homosexual'. Kenneth Leech makes an important point:

> Much discussion of sexuality starts from an idealistic approach about what should be rather than a realist or historical materialist analysis of what is. So the rhetoric of sexuality often fails to connect with the reality of people's lives and loves ... The persistence of idealist views of sexuality makes a Christian engagement with the realities of flesh and human passion more difficult and creates a spirituality which is several removes from the human condition.[1]

So let me start by saying what is a realistic view of homosexuality. To be homosexual is simply to be someone who, without any particular wish or intention, finds as he or she grows up that physical and emotional attachment is stronger towards his or her own sex than towards the opposite sex. This does not mean that very close friendships may not be formed with the opposite sex (in fact, because there is no physical threat, friendships with married women or married men can be more secure and restful to them), but it does mean that sexually the homosexual will be drawn towards his or her own sex. This is not an expression of perversity nor is it born from a deliberate desire to 'sin'; it is simply an expression of what *is* – the reality of the situation. To be homosexual is not necessarily to be effeminate or to be trans-sexual in dress or attitudes – transvestism is found as often amongst heterosexuals, and in these days of 'uni-sex' clothing, many women wear men's trousers, although we do not yet give the same tolerance to men wearing skirts, except to Scotsmen and clergymen!

How or why the homosexual orientation is developed is not definitely known: some speak of hormone imbalance, others think it a result of over-possessiveness, or alternatively of total coldness in affection, on the part of one or other of the parents. But we are concerned with facts rather than causation. The facts are that a sizeable proportion of human beings, usually estimated at about 10 per cent, are predominantly homosexual and many others are bisexual. Homosexuality is neither an illness nor a deviation (since the word 'deviation' implies a wilful turning from what is normal), nor would it necessarily be much of a problem (it has not been in some other cultures) were it not subject to social and religious condemnation. The homosexual has not entered upon a way of life deliberately chosen. (Some priests, as confessors, used to urge that marriage would change the orientation; this is not only untrue but has often led to disastrous marriages.) The homosexual has found himself or herself in an orientation of life that can be changed no more than can that of a heterosexual; it appears to him or her to be the God-given reality of his or her nature, and therefore to be accepted as such.

It does not follow that sexual desire in a homosexual is less strong than in a heterosexual person, nor that compulsory celibacy is the answer. As I have said before, it has always surprised me that a church which teaches rightly that celibacy is a high and voluntary vocation – a sacrifice undertaken in order that some more overwhelming purpose may be fulfilled, as presumably lay behind the choice made by Christ and many of the great saints – should also demean the whole concept of celibacy by making it an enforced rule for every homosexual, as indeed for every unmarried person. The three great virtues of monasticism – poverty, celibacy and obedience – lose all value if they are enforced rather than chosen by the grace of God; the church has never supported a compelled poverty or a compelled obedience, so why a compelled celibacy?

2. Having then considered, with reality rather than fantasy, what is meant by being homosexual, we should apply the basic sexual ethic I have outlined in chapter 17. As every human being is made in the image of God, if that theology of creative wholeness is to be applied to the homosexual, what will be the maximum degree of fulfilment of body, mind and spirit within the limitations of that condition? Helmut Thielecke gives a realistic answer to that question:

> Perhaps the best way to formulate the ethical problem of the constitutional homosexual, who because of his vitality is not able to practise abstinence, is to ask whether within the co-ordinating system of his constitution he is willing to structure the man/man relationship in an ethically responsible way ... the homosexual has to realise his optimal ethical responsibilities on the basis of his irreversible situation. Celibacy cannot be used as a counter-argument because celibacy is based upon a special calling and, moreover, is an act of free-will.[2] [This passage could equally well be written using feminine instead of masculine language.]

There is more mature common sense and understanding in these few remarks than in most ethical judgements from the churches on this subject. Thielecke is saying that a good,

126

sound and loving homosexual relationship is far more likely to produce the best than a repressed, enforced celibacy, which may well lead either to great loneliness and unfilled need to love or to a furtive promiscuity hidden from the world, with all the likely ensuing disasters of scandal or disease.

One would have thought this was obvious common sense, but it seems not yet to be accepted by the church. If the Christian religion teaches that we should be true to ourselves, then it seems strange that those who 'come out' in society with honesty about themselves should be victimised, while those who hide behind a false exterior are encouraged. The church, particularly in relation to its priests, sometimes gives the impression that it prefers dishonesty and secrecy rather than openness – a very odd view for a church which preaches that 'perfect love casts out fear'!

3. If we are made in the image of God we are also always becoming what we are meant to be. Thielecke also points out that homosexuality, like most other facts of human behaviour which are not chosen but are conditioned by circumstances, falls into the category not of concrete sin but of original sin – part of the pattern of the fallen world:

> The homosexual potentiality dare not be any more strongly depreciated than the status of existence in which we all share as man in the disordered creation that exists since the Fall. Consequently there is not the slightest excuse for maligning the constitutional homosexual morally or theologically. We are all under the same condemnation and each of us has received his 'share' of it.[3]

So like everything else in life we should be encouraged to make the best of what we are but, as Kenneth Leech says: 'Human experience shows that sexual relationships are enormously varied and do not conform to, or deviate from, a simple norm.'[4] Homosexual relationships can be judged by the same criteria as other sexual relationships: quite obviously a sexual act which is simply the satisfaction of physical desire and has no intention of any kind of real relationship is at the bottom of the scale of human values; equally obviously long-term relationships offering love and stability throughout life are at the maximum level of fulfilment. But many human beings fall somewhere between these two. If, as we are finding, even heterosexual marriage is breaking down more frequently despite all the support of society, children and home, then can we expect greater stability from relationships which have none of these? I am constantly surprised that, despite no social or church approval, many homosexual relationships achieve a loyalty, love and stability greater than many marriages. This is admirable and should, one would think, win the support and encouragement of the church as the best outcome in the circumstances.

There are, as Leech says, many levels of relationship in life, and we are called to the optimal potentiality within these levels. The spirit of truth calls us to have reverence for fact and reality, to live by the deepest reality of which we are capable and to know at what level of reality we are capable of living.

Perhaps the guidelines offered by Norman Pittenger for homosexuals are as real an ethic as we can find:

(1) No one should accept his homosexuality without questioning it.

(2) If he recognises that he is homosexual he should gladly accept it as his condition.

(3) God will help the homosexual to be the best he can be, so seek God's help.

(4) Exercise strong self-control in sexual advances to others.

(5) Make friends in the same ways as do all others.

(6) If a homosexual is in love, it must be tested by the normal criteria, and may only take physical expression in a truly 'loving' relationship.[5]

(I presume Pittenger would suggest the same guidelines for lesbians.) Some, however, might find even these guidelines verging on the ideal rather than the real, but it is never bad to have an ideal so long as it is recognised for what it is.

128

4. We are called in all things to measure our maturity by Christ. Christ teaches us little about sexuality but much about the quality and nature of love. He shows us that love is costly and vulnerable and is usually found through some kind of death. Although some homosexuals do achieve lasting relationships there will be many more who, like myself, do not. The homosexual will usually have to face loneliness, the experience of rejected love, the lessening of the likelihood of lasting and good relationships as he grows older. He will not find much support from other homosexuals, either because of their fear or because of their own persistent and usually unavailing search for 'the perfect lover' or eternal 'youth'. But all these facts, and the awareness of belonging to a despised minority, need not cause any self-pity but can bring great value to oneself and to others. There are various reasons for this:

(a) Belonging to a minority can help one towards greater understanding and sensitivity to other minorities. I have always found that my natural tendency in politics, in religion and in matters of race and sexism, is to be with the minority.
(b) The experience of living alone enables one to realise that aloneness need not mean loneliness and to offer understanding to some of the many people in our society who live alone – either from choice or through circumstances.
(c) If a one-to-one relationship is denied, then more and deeper friendships may be formed and a less inclusive life than is sometimes found with those whose horizons often seem bound by marriage and the nuclear family. As a priest I have often had a greater flexibility and availability than many married clergy who necessarily have to give a considerable degree of time to their family. Many of the finest priests in the inner city have been, by orientation, 'gay'.

I have given considerable space to matters of marriage and divorce and to homosexuality, and to rethinking the church's attitudes to these matters, because the first is the most general problem with which the church has to deal and the second is a matter in which I have a personal interest and which is also a much-talked-of subject in the church and in society at the present time. I shall turn now to consider, more briefly, one other matter which comes within the sphere of sexuality and has been much discussed in the church in recent years.

1 Kenneth Leech, in an article in the *Independent*, taken from an essay in *Embracing the Chaos*, SPCK 1990.
2 Helmut Thielecke, *The Ethics of Sex* (James Clarke 1964), pp. 284–5.
3 Ibid., p. 283.
4 Leech, op. cit.
5 Norman Pittenger, *Time for Consent* (SCM Press 1976), quoted in R. Jones, *Groundwork of Christian Ethics* (Epworth Press 1984), p. 131.

20

ORDINATION OF WOMEN

For long I resisted the ordination of women on the grounds first of what I believed to be doctrine and then for ecumenical reasons. I have been slowly led to see that what I thought of as doctrine was really a thinly veiled male chauvinism and misunderstanding of the meaning of human sexuality in the purposes of God. As Don Cupitt says:

> The connexion between God, masculinity, form and the rational soul on the one hand and between woman, matter and corruptibility on the other was built into philosophy, science and theology at their inception. It is undeniable that Western thought from the beginning has been applied sexism.[1]

Although it is quite clear that gender cannot be an attribute of God, since God is neither male nor female but spirit, in all theological writings, from the ancient Hebrew onwards, God has been seen as a male, and woman as subservient to man.

As a result, instead of thinking of Christ as representing God in humanity, emphasis has been laid upon the essential maleness of Christ. For a long time I colluded with the idea that women could not be ordained because as Christ the original priest was, in gender, male there was something essentially male about the priesthood. The fact that this was pleasing to my own subconscious feeling of the superiority of the male may also have motivated me more than I cared to acknowledge.

Later I came to see that my attitude to the ordination of women was in fact revealing a great deal about myself. A deeper understanding of the meaning of 'in Christ there is

no male or female' has led me to see that the true represen-
tation of Christ is not that of maleness but of the act of
creation, of the oneness of male and female in the human,
of the presence of the masculine and feminine in every
one of us. The church has in general been content to continue the stereotypes of the male (the virile, power-centred
role, dominant and hierarchical) and the female (the passive, serving, sacrificing), and we have let these stereotypes
lead us, at times in the church's history, into some of the
worst misunderstandings and practices of male domination.
A true understanding of the doctrine of the *theotokos*, or
'Mother of God' as applied to Mary, takes us beyond these
stereotypes into the elevation of the whole of humankind as
male and female persons in God's creative and saving act,
in absolute union and deep qualitative equality, and also
enables us to see Christ as representing not maleness as a
gender but the importance of a humanity which is also
divine – a humanity that reflects the masculine–feminine in
every one of us, and also something of the power–powerlessness of God.

By electing Mary to incarnate Christ, God elected what is
tender, loving and personifying in his creation and rejected
the virile, masculine role. In the saving act of God in
Christ the female–male are united in the one human being
which is both, where the masculine acts of resolution by
power, possession and force are rejected and the feminine
acts are accepted – the self-offering sacrifice of the Lamb of
God like the self-offering of the woman that new life may
be born. (It seems to me that the ordination of women could
make a great difference in encouraging an understanding of
evangelism as neither power-centred nor campaign-centred
but centred instead in self-offering love. This is, of course,
assuming that the women ordained are not the kind who
think they have to pretend to be and act like dominating
males!)

Two Roman Catholic theologians, one Greek Orthodox
and the other Roman Catholic, put this point of view very
strongly. Nikos Nissiotis, Professor of Theology at the University of Athens, writes:

The elevation and exaltation of Mary as *theotokos* can illustrate a new approach to the priority of the female element... Consequently the *theotokos* can also influence all structures of the church, rendering its ministry more charismatic and flexible, taking away its despotism, clericalism, and false male ministerial functionalism.[2]

The Roman Catholic theologian, a woman at the University of Nijmegen, Catharina Halkes, says:

If we continue to cling literally to the femininity of Mary and the masculinity of Jesus, neither women nor the community of the church will move... in the mystery of the Incarnation which was a divine and human event two people were involved at the deepest level – the male Jesus and the female Mary. Because of this the life-giving divine revelation at the centre of the Christian faith should not be allowed to become ossified according to parts played by man or woman, with the result that a woman cannot sacramentally mediate salvation... it needs hardly to be said that male and female no longer exist in the reality of God's revelation and that we are all one in Christ. But this is not yet a reality and we must all learn to advance towards it: it is only when the church is bold enough to look at every aspect of the great Mother that full justice will be done to women and a sound Mariology will be able to have a salutary effect on women as well as on men.[3]

It is very strange and a paradox that the main body of the Roman Catholic Church, which has always rightly exalted the place of Mary, has not been able to see in her the liberating fiat from a dominating masculinity in ministry. The churches in Latin America do see this and rightly see in her the prophet of liberation theology.

The masculine ego-consciousness that separates itself from the feminine will never find completeness. It can become a complete human being only if it realises its own feminine element. In Mary is seen the autonomy of the feminine, the self-offering of the feminine, the true purpose of a human being as that of servant to the poor and the oppressed, the liberator from stereotypes of male and female. In other words, the whole human being grows together out of the contradictions of feminine and masculine, unconscious and conscious, earthly and divine.

I believe that the Roman Catholic Church of the future, including as it will a much larger proportion of its membership from Latin America and the Third World, will come to see the implications of both Marian theology and Christology and will then begin to question whether its structures reflect its theology. I hope this is already happening in those parts of the Anglican Church in which women are already being ordained and will in England too, now that the General Synod has passed the legislation which will lead to the ordination of women to the priesthood. This is, I believe, a great step forward to the true understanding of priesthood, for the following reasons:

(a) It will release priesthood from being tied to gender and enable us to see Christ as representing humanity rather than masculinity.

(b) It will bring into the priesthood the qualities of both male and female, thus enabling it to provide a much more comprehensive ministry.

(c) It will enable the Anglican Church to spend time on its true mission to extend the kingdom of God rather than on purely ecclesiastical matters.

It is sad that there are some who cannot accept a decision which, after years of careful debate, supposedly inspired by the Holy Spirit, they knew had to be taken. The Church of England has been known for its capacity to hold together people having widely differing understanding of questions of fundamental importance, and usually over the years a reasonably happy coexistence has been possible. Why should ordination of women be the one question of such gravity as to make schism in the Anglican Communion justifiable? In reality, ordination of women is neither a matter of doctrine nor of feminism but a true understanding of sexuality – of the unity and complementary equality of the male and female, both outwardly in society and inwardly within ourselves.

1 Don Cupitt, *Radicals and the Future of the Church* (SCM Press 1989), p. 45.
2 'Mary in the Churches', *Concilium* (T. and T. Clark October 1983), pp. 35, 36.
3 Ibid., pp. 69, 71, 73.

21

MAKING COMMUNITY INTO A REALITY

I mentioned in chapter 15 that Bishop John Taylor regarded one of the prime functions of the church to be a therapeutic fellowship in which each member learns to be fearlessly open to the rest and so both gives and receives healing and support.

But such supportive communities will not happen unless we deliberately create them. A church which sees itself primarily as a liturgical group meeting once a week for worship of the kind and nature acceptable to the worshipper will never become the kind of community John Taylor envisages nor one like that of which the early church gives us a vision: 'Now the company of those who believed were of one heart and soul, and no one said that any of the things which he possessed was his own, but they had everything in common' (Acts 4:32 RSV). Moltmann says of this vision, 'I do not see this as a utopia but rather as a divine promise of the Spirit which we too can experience.'[1] Nevertheless, if such a vision of community in the church is to be experienced there are many hard obstacles to be overcome, some of which I outlined in chapter 11.

First, there is the tendency towards increasing centralisation in our society. If the Anglican Church follows this lead and tries to deal with its problems by increasing centralisation, how is it to build up the grass-roots communities by which alone a humanness is given to all this centralised structure? And how is the church to have both a ministry to the world on the larger canvas and yet fulfil its equally true function to be locally the Body of Christ, intricately and intimately bound together as are the members of the human body? The church has been described as 'a community of brethren' which

> ... goes further than an assembly of believers for the purpose of proclaiming the gospel and partaking in the sacraments ... and embraces the whole of life, our dealings with one another, our representation for others and our common actions. The 'community of brethren' means the new, visible way of life. In the New Testament this is often contrasted with social conditions in the surrounding world.[2]

WHAT IS CHRISTIAN COMMUNITY?

There can be no doubt that the churches' task in this increasingly non-communal world is to rebuild community and to be itself a community. But that immediately raises questions, each of which I shall be concerned with as I look to the future of the church. The first and most important question is: what do we mean by Christian community? From this arise other questions:

(i) What kind of community? Among the different kinds of community there are those whose main function is to provide mutual support for its members, those which are formed in order to promote responsible action for the promotion of the kingdom of God and the needs of the area, and those both within and outside the church which are related to pastoral care, especially in relation to various groups and people in need of special care.

(ii) What form of organisation will be required for different areas and parishes? For example, in the small parish the church community can be very central to the life of the whole village community, while in large urban parishes the church may well have to train its members to act within specialised groups within the area. In other words the function of an urban church will be to bring the understanding of what is meant by community, whether of action or support, into already existing communal groupings.

I think the difference between the natural groupings of like background, tastes and social recreation which form in every area and the Christian understanding of community lies in the depth of the fellowship and the motivation behind the formation of these groups. A doctor in a therapeutic hospital once wrote: 'It seems to me that our greatest need is for the development of the churches as centres of living fellowship where the essence of the gospel communicates itself by virtue of its total atmosphere and environment.'

It is this depth communication which is lacking in most churches. The reality is more likely to be that a group of people gather together once a week for worship and within that group natural friendships or associations form. There is often little difference between the groupings formed within the church and those outside; in both, the groups will be largely of similar ethnic, age and class background. There is nothing wrong with this and it is perfectly natural that like should go with like, but there is probably little movement between one group and another, and there is nothing specially Christian about such groupings. It would be difficult to see how 'the essence of the gospel' is 'communicating itself', and it would be equally difficult to see any new visible way of life.

STEPS IN BUILDING CHRISTIAN COMMUNITY

If, then, the future church is to develop greater depth in its understanding and practice of Christian community, the following changes in parish life need to take place:

1. Every effort must be made within the structure of parish life and organisation to enable members of the church to know each other, 'warts and all', at much greater depth than at present, so that we can be aware of those people needing support and the possible areas of conflict in relationships.

There is often in church congregations a superficiality of relationship which is far removed from the true and realistic understanding of love. A stereotype of 'niceness' often takes

138

the place of loving and caring, and equally fixed ideas of the importance of 'respectability' and 'conformity' often prevent us from being able to accept badness as well as goodness, in ourselves and in others. This also means that we often cannot face the reality of conflict and we either skate around it or try to ignore it, feeling that we cannot have a 'flaming' row with the vicar or another member of the church without having to leave it! The view frequently held is that being a Christian means never having a row or expressing strong feelings, on the grounds that we must not 'hurt' people. No one seems to have noticed that Jesus himself had no hesitation in expressing very strong feelings; if I had been a Pharisee or a rich man I would have felt very hurt by some of the things said of me and to me by Jesus, according to the gospel records.

This attitude often causes the church to appear capable only of dealing with people who conform to the general social pattern of the neighbourhood; those who are different are felt to be difficult and made to feel unwelcome. Someone once said that the average church would find it equally difficult to deal with a cat-burglar or a saint as a member of its congregation and that many churches were more interested in being a respectable community than a redeemed community. This is certainly true in my own experience in suburbia and now in West Sussex.

But this is no one's fault. It is simply that the usual church organisation does not give the opportunities for recognising and coming to terms with the deeper and sometimes darker level of our personalities. Christopher Bryant says there is

> ... the inevitable conflict between what the individual is or feels himself to be and what society expects him to be. This tension between the individual and society begins in infancy and continues through life ... We all have to suppress something of ourselves in order to be acceptable to society. In practice the individual learns to adopt a manner ... which both expresses and conceals what we are.[3]

But if this is true within the church then we will never have a Christian community, only a pseudo-community of people not as we are but as we want to be seen. If the local church really wants to become a Christian community it will move from the present ordering of the weekday church life into women's groups, men's groups and youth groups based on a speaker or recreational activity and instead find room for relatively small groups meeting without any agenda save that which they themselves bring from their own lives and problems. Such groups would be small, because only so would members really get to know each other and give everyone within the group the chance to reveal themselves without embarrassment.

It is no accident that Jesus worked with twelve disciples – the modern group leader would regard twelve as about the right number for a group which is to fulfil the purpose of knowing and understanding each other. This is the kind of therapeutic group providing support and openness described by John Taylor (see chapter 15). He writes: ' . . . the essential unit in which the church exists must be small enough to enable all its members to find one another in mutual awareness yet large enough for them to be an embodiment of the life of the kingdom.'[4]

My suggestion would be that as many as possible of the congregation should be involved in these groups over limited periods (e.g. using university and school terms as the period of meeting) and for the purposes of deeper knowing and sharing I described in chapter 6 for support groups. After a period those groups should be broken up and re-formed with other members of the congregation. Clergy and laity should take part in these groups on equal terms; in no sense should the clergy act as leaders or chairpersons. In this way, in the course of time, there would develop a far more profound knowledge of each other within a congregation, and much would have been learnt as to how to deal with conflicts, dislikes, prejudices, judgementalism and anger – all these things would have been experienced in the group at first hand. Trust would grow, there would be less hesitation to share personal problems, clergy would be seen to be as fallible as laity, and both would learn to recognise 'hidden agenda' at business meetings to be as important as written agenda. What is now superficial would become real 'speaking the truth in love', and this new under-standing learned of what community truly is would then indeed be the Gospel communicating itself to other com-munities in the secular world with which the church mem-bers are involved.

2. Another function of the local church as community is the function of promoting necessary responsible action to meet both the political, social and personal needs of people within the area. This may necessitate the ignoring of parish bound-aries and thinking in terms of an area rather than a parish. I remind you here of the third function seen by John Taylor as a task of a Christian community: ' . . . a dynamically res-ponsible fellowship which enables its members to rise to their full human potential and to engage positively in chang-ing that area of the world's life for which, under God, they take responsibility'.[5]

We always have to remember that it is not *going* to church that is important but rather *being* the church in one's local area, standing for that which Christ proclaimed as the mani-festo of the kingdom when he took over the words of Isaiah and made them his own:

> He will not fail or be discouraged till he has established justice in the earth; and the coastlands wait for his law . . . I have given you as a covenant to the people, a light to the nations, to open the eyes that are blind, to bring out the prisoners from the dungeon, from the prison those who sit in darkness. (Isaiah 42:4, 6–8 RSV)

The church community has then a dual function if it is to be the instrument of God's kingdom in the world:

(a) To recognise that in the corporate life of human beings the word 'love' stands for 'justice'. Therefore both the national and the local church will be constantly vigilant to see that justice is done, in national and in local affairs. On the larger canvas of national life this may well have to be as in secular society, through those delegated from below or elected from below to represent the Anglican Church in the General Synod and its various boards which cover all areas of national life. In the local area the wise church will make an audit of the area so that it may be clear what are the needs of justice in such matters as housing, unemployment, ethnic and sexual minorities, and the care of the old and the disabled. Then, if the church is to equip itself properly for the work which is seen to need most responsible action, the church community has to decide who is best fitted to take the lead in whatever action is necessary and, perhaps, to train him or her or them in how to set in force responsible action and to know what support they will need in doing this. The church has to examine its

> ... liberation, salvation-creating action from the point of view of the people and their interests ... consequently the action of the church should not merely be directed towards the people but should also, and above all, permit itself to be directed by the people.[6]

It is foolish to say, as is often said, that the church should not interfere in politics. The church has no alternative to interfering in politics, for politics is the instrument of justice or injustice, and the way by which love is expressed in the world is primarily through justice. Moreover, the whole concept of the kingdom of God for which we pray each time we say the Lord's Prayer means nothing if it is not concerned with the hope of a future world which will reflect God's will and purpose more than is so at present. The hope of the kingdom of God is an eschatological hope which must be the ever-present task of the Christian community to bring about. As Moltmann says:

> The salvation which faith embraces in hope is therefore not a private but a public salvation, not only spiritual but also bodily, not a purely religious but also a political salvation. We may not separate this into two kingdoms but must recognise the cruciform character of this Saviour and his salvation in all its dimensions of life.[7]

A Christian community will see itself as continuously working within its area, and sometimes on the larger canvas of national life, for:

(i) human rights and freedom of information so that oppression can be resisted and cover-up avoided;

(ii) human solidarity against division of race from race, class from class, one sexual orientation from another, old from young, and the alienation of disabled and elderly people;

(iii) human economic justice against extremes of riches and poverty;

(iv) human future against ecological destruction and pollution;

(v) human hope and peace against depression, stress and the pile-up of nuclear weapons and the arms trade.

(b) While continuously working for a world which more clearly resembles the kingdom of God, the second function of a Christian community is to recognise our identification with the suffering and crucified Christ and, by that identification, to be aware of and identified with the many in our midst who are suffering in body, mind or spirit – often caused largely through the insensitivity of the world around them.

As a society we are rapidly becoming more ready to dispose of things and people; added to an in-built obsolescence of things, there appears to be now in relationships a similar obsolescence time towards people. It shows itself in many different ways. Some marriages break down because change is now seen as a quality more to be desired than permanence and difficulties as something to escape from rather than resolve. We move away from an area and old friendships die; soon the only contact is the Christmas card.

All too often we are unaware of what is happening within our own area. I have often noticed that members of the congregation often do not know of the trouble being faced by those mentioned in the intercessions. Fewer of the clergy visit as a matter of regularity; in the area in which I live only one parish priest regularly visits his people – the others seem to be preoccupied with their meetings, committees and other matters. So it is no longer possible to rely on the parish priest for information concerning the old, the ill or the lonely, or who is under stress or having personal difficulties. Widows are often left out of dinner invitations after their husbands have died; why? They surely need the company more then.

Are we willing to share financially with members of our church who have fallen into money difficulties as a result of unemployment or business failures or fraud? I remember when we had meetings of those who had lost sums of money, some of them considerable, in the Barlow Clowes scandal (I was one, although I lost less than many others). They reported that, although many of them belonged to churches and lived in parishes where there were people of great wealth, they had received no offers of loans or gifts to tide over difficulties. They received much verbal sympathy but very little practical sharing.

I once had a personal experience, to my own shame, of how easy it is to live in ignorance of need very near at hand. I had often preached on the need to be with others in the loneliness of old age, while I was unaware that only four doors from me lived an old man nearly housebound with no near relations and few callers. When eventually I heard about him I did then call. I was immediately welcomed, and the warmth was reciprocal; I had found someone near who lived alone as I did, and with whom I could have a drink and talk of an evening.

This then is the other side of practising Christian community: to spend some time with the old, the lonely, the housebound; to invite the single person, especially those made so by bereavement, to share a meal; to inquire of those who will know needs in our area (medical and social service workers) what kinds of help are needed and then respond to those needs as a church or as a member within a church or, if the needs require specialist training, to be willing as groups or individuals to undergo the training required. The world does not need unskilled and often insensitive 'do-gooders', but it does need those who are prepared to give time to be trained in the art of counselling effectively. And who should be more ready to give that time than those whose gospel is based upon love and human relationship? Many areas of human difficulty require skilled counselling: bereavement, living alone, stress, marriage breakdown, sexual problems, coping with conflict, anger and failure, and also long-term and terminal illness.

There are also the various difficulties which people face at each age of life – childhood, adolescence, young adulthood, middle age, old age – difficulties which will be found in every parish. If the church has learned what community means, then members of the church can be of great value to each other and to other parishioners in sharing the problems they have in common. It is of course true that many of these problems may be also dealt with by voluntary organisations and local authority departments, and it would be foolish of the church to work on its own rather than with them, but it would be of great help to the re-establishment of supportive community life if the local church were to do a great deal more than it does at present towards the promotion of true community. Moltmann emphasises this point:

> We have taken mission, ecumenical relationships and diaconia from local communities and delegated them to large organisations. This has made the local community poor and passive. The delegation of tasks which one can do oneself leads to alienation. So we are returning these tasks to the local community in order that local communities can be diaconal, missionary and ecumenical. The local communities can themselves care for many of their handicapped and old members once they become living communities instead of religious liturgical communities.[8]

Last, but not least, we have often failed to be a true community because we have concentrated on 'coming to church'. We have thought that getting people inside a building once a week is Christian community. We have not realised the truth of John Robinson's comment that 'there is no holy communion without holy community'.

Perhaps the most important reality that has to be radically faced, if there is to be true grass-roots authority from below rather than from above, is the fundamental reordering of the structures of the church. This is sufficiently important for the subject to be treated in a separate chapter.

1 Jurgen Moltmann, *Creating a Just Future* (SCM Press 1989), p. 9.
2 Jurgen Moltmann, *The Church in the Power of the Spirit* (SCM Press 1977), p. 315.
3 Christopher Bryant, *Jung and the Christian Way* (Darton, Longman and Todd 1983), pp. 69, 70.
4 John V. Taylor, *The Church Reshaped* (CMS 1975), p. 14.
5 Ibid.
6 Medellin Conclusions 1968.
7 Jurgen Moltmann, *On Human Dignity* (SCM Press 1984), p. 104.
8 Moltmann, *Creating a Just Future*, p. 10.

22

STRUCTURES TO FACILITATE COMMUNITY IN THE CHURCH

One of the difficulties which has never been properly resolved, either in the church or in other groupings in society, political and economic, is how leadership which grows from below and is properly located within the grass roots of society can be formed and made realistically effective. In society we talk of democracy but this finds little scope in the occasional voting in of representatives to parliament and local councils. To change things from below often becomes very difficult once a group obtains a secure majority; and in the world of economics and business, money and power reside in the hands of the few who have gained that power by their wealth rather than by process of popular election.

STRUCTURES OF CLERICAL AND LAY LEADERSHIP

In the Anglican Church it has never been resolved what kind of leadership we are looking for. It is constantly pointed out that the church does not claim to be a democracy but is, rather, a hierarchy in which authority, unity and community are expressed through bishops, to the clergy, to the laity rather than the other way round. The bishop is variously described (in the Report of the Lambeth Conference of 1978) as a father-in-God to his diocese over which he exercises pastoral care and especially to the clergy; he is the sign and agent of unity within the whole church and his authority is expressed through his leadership and participation in the synods and councils of the church. It is manifestly clear, however, that in practice none of these descriptions is realistic or accurate. On this subject Gerald Priestland has written:

> Since human organisation demands leadership, we must get bishops (or moderators) back to what they were in the Celtic church – not committee men and administrators but evangelists and saints. I know some very holy bishops today, but they find it hard to fit in their diaries.[1]

I am not sure whether we can expect from the bishop any more than from the clergy or laity the perfectionism of the saint, but if any of the descriptions given in that Lambeth Report are to be reality rather than fantasy some very different concepts of the office of bishop are needed. Similarly, there needs to be new thinking about the role of priests and of the laity.

The role of bishops

If the bishop is to be father-in-God to the clergy and laity then obviously the area of his episcopacy needs to be much smaller; it is not possible to be a pastoral father to all the clergy in a large area, where the most the clergy will see of him is a few times each year and then usually on official liturgical occasions like inductions or confirmations. As for the laity, they will rarely, if ever, even speak to their bishop. There is a limit to the number of people with whom a pastoral relationship can be made.

Moreover, if the bishop is to be a father-in-God to his clergy he must present a very different image to that often given today. In many cases the bishop seems to want to distance himself from his clergy, to be a remote and rather unapproachable figure wrapped in some mantle of awesome authority to which others are expected to bow! It is said of some bishops who find communication difficult that they are 'shy', but that is somewhat feeble; a person who has to

148

communicate from a position of pastoral care and authority cannot afford to be 'shy' and must learn either to overcome such a psychological disadvantage or refuse to be appointed to such a position. It seems to me that, despite the difficulties, we need today to lessen the social status and remote authority of the bishop as a near-monarchical figure, and to increase his viability and availability, so that the parish priest can have a reciprocal relationship – to receive and give support.

It is often said, and rightly, as a reason against the creation of smaller dioceses, that if the structure of synods and administration is to be reproduced in each diocese this would mean a great increase in bureaucracy and expense. But why cannot administrative structure be separated from pastoral oversight? Could not several small dioceses have a joint administrative and synodical structure coterminous with the areas of local and national authority and thus enable each diocesan bishop to do his real pastoral work within a smaller area and also relieve him of much administration? Thus the administrative authority of the bishop would be lessened, but his spiritual authority increased through greater opportunities for pastoral care and oversight.

It is also untrue to say that the bishop is the focus of unity of the whole church. In actual fact most bishops, by claiming the right to be the supreme authority in the diocese, undermine the unity of the whole, since one diocese will have one set of rules and policies differing from those in another; the differences will lie in the views of the two bishops rather than in any differences between the grass-roots community of the whole church in each diocese. We are already seeing this in the divisiveness between one diocese and another regarding the position of women in local ministry, and these differences between dioceses and bishops will increase when women are ordained to the priesthood.

If there are to be such major differences in policy and attitude between one diocese and another, then it is foolish to talk of the bishop as the focus for unity of the whole church. As for a bishop expressing his authority through his leadership and participation in the synods of the church, if this means that the synods are simply to be – as indeed they often are – expressions of the views and policies of the bishops, then this is clearly contrary to the understanding of corporate community. It would be more fitting for the position of the bishop in this structure to be more like that of the sovereign, a figurehead to carry out the policies worked out communally through the synods elected from the local communities. What is needed in the future church is an increase in the number of bishops able, through jurisdiction over smaller numbers, to be true fathers-in-God and resources of spiritual and pastoral care, alongside a lessening of episcopal policy and administrative authority. Perhaps then we should have the vision of the bishops as the evangelists and saints that Gerald Priestland called for!

The role of priests

This pattern of increased priesthood and less clericalism should also go right through the ministries of the church. When I worked with Cecilia Goodenough in lay training she had great respect for priesthood but a great antipathy to clericalism. She said that the only reason she might oppose the ordination of women was if it would add to the numbers who deserted the laity for the status of clergy. If I thought this to be true I would agree, but I hope that women are not going to copy men who only feel secure when robed in a cassock or a black suit and clerical collar; in fact I hope that women deacons will soon stop wearing clerical collars and find some symbol of pastoral care more suitable to the body and dress of women – perhaps a revival of the elegant lace stock of the old days!

There is still far too much clericalism expected by many of the clergy and meekly accepted by the laity; this is destructive of true community. The policy of the parish is not the prerogative of the parish priest, and therefore to be changed with each successive incumbent, nor should the laity be always waiting for the priest to take the initiative in what should be done in the parish. As with the bishop, the priest should be the theological resource person, the pastoral friend and guide in his parish, not the person who decides about the future policy of the local church and then imposes that policy on the laity or manipulates them into accepting it. True community is never built up by dependence, only by interdependence.

The role of the laity

Similar words of warning must also be given to the laity. There can be lay domination, either by a powerful figure or patron, or by a group, a kind of local mafia, and this is as ruinous of true community as is episcopal or clerical domination. It is important that varying ages and interests be represented in policy-making in the church, otherwise it will be dominated, as I am afraid it often is, by the ideas simply of one generation. If this is the older generation, as is often so, the local church will become a focus of conservative traditionalism looking ever backwards to the past with nostalgia rather than forwards to the future life and vitality of the Gospel. We live in a sequence of successive generations, and if there is to be true community there must be interdependence in ideas and authority, looking always to express the text of the Gospel within the context of society and also within the context of every generation of society, not just the old or the young.

At present congregations often seem to swing between those who in music and worship are always looking backwards and those who imagine that in order to attract the young we must all be subjected to the kind of chorus, disco, 'clap-happy' style. Both of these are ephemeral. What is really needed is to understand and be able to minister to the deeper needs, problems and joys of the young, the middle-aged and the old. If there are too few young in our local church to be able to listen at first hand to those needs, then we must research into the world outside the church through groups who are prepared to listen in the community to what different generations are saying and thinking.

Developing new ministerial structures

'If the truth is to reach men and women through the spirit of the Christian community then the organisation and structure of that community must be adapted to establish a living continuity with them.'[2] This statement by John Baker is very true, but has the structure of the Church of England been adapted to this end? From its earliest days the Church of England has been structured into parishes, each with its priest and its church together focusing the connection between Christian community and local community. Given the right sense of pastoral care by church members and parson, this worked in a general way so long as England was a network of relatively small towns and villages, but since the Industrial Revolution the growth of large towns has made nonsense of the parish as a focus of community or of the priest as the 'parson', the 'person' in the place. In all the town parishes in which I have served, the 'parish' has been an arbitrary selection of streets, with no recognisable distinction in boundary or character between one parish and another. As a result the church has often become not the parish church but an 'associational' church of people who subscribe to a particular emphasis in doctrine and policy or have preferences in forms of worship – so emerged the 'low' and 'high' churches and now the charismatic church.

How arbitrary and lacking in any real connection between parish and local community the structure has become is obvious when we try to apply parish boundaries to weddings and baptisms. No couple understands, nor should they, why they have to be married or have their children baptised in a particular building when they would prefer one only two or three streets away.

In ministerial organisation the church has dealt with declining numbers by taking clergy away from villages and scattering them through the towns, but in such a way that they become lost in the massive population of a so-called 'urban parish'. The unsatisfactory situation of many rural parishes now deprived of local priests has been described in chapter 11, and this policy, in the opinion of many, has been a mistake. It is only in a village where the local priest is able to be a true parson, knowing his people through the social and political interrelationships of a small community and through the systematic visiting which is possible when he has less than five hundred parishioners in his care. As a young man I spent much time in a Devon village and could see what opportunities were open to a good priest. Only once in my own ministry had I anything resembling a village, and that was a commuter village of nearly two thousand inhabitants in Surrey. Even with that number (many of whom were there for only part of the week) I was able to achieve more personal knowledge of the whole community, as distinct from just the Christian community, than in any other of the much larger parishes of which I was vicar. There is still therefore much sense in having one person in each small community who can be the focus for the relationship of the church to that community. If it is not possible to reverse the policy and have a vicar or rector in each village – and I admit that, unless numbers greatly increase or the ordination of women as priests brings many more into the stipendiary ministry, this is likely to be the case – then, since one person in one place is a good principle, much more use must be made of non-stipendiary or local clergy. If in each village one member, who is well respected and holds responsible secular work in the community – perhaps a local shopkeeper, farmer, teacher, publican or a retired but still active person – would come forward and be accepted for ordination with such necessary liturgical and doctrinal training as is appropriate to the function of president of the Eucharist and preacher, then it could still be possible for each village to have its priest. I shall be developing this idea in later chapters.

With regard to towns, here the importance of ministerial structure depends not on distinguishing between the ordained and the lay but on using the capacities for leadership available within the area. Indeed, we may well be thinking here of the area rather than the parish, since in some areas there will be a considerable range of different types of indigenous leadership and in other areas, where the inhabitants of the area are more accustomed to being dependent than to being initiators, there will be little. Here, then, the real way forward is through lay training, for it is only if the laity consciously see themselves as exercising a mission within the area of their secular work or groups in the area that the church will have any influence. I quoted earlier (in chapter 3) from an article by Ruth Etchells: she continued with these words:

> Such lay ministers ought to be commissioned by their parishes and sent out to their task and then supported by weekly prayer for them in the parish church, by counselling and by support groups (within which they can share problems). But their function is not to keep the church going as an institution but to draw their support, comfort, sustenance and theological depth from it as they work in Christ's name in their secular calling.[3]

In this work of lay leadership the reverse will be true of what is often supposed. Such lay leaders will not be there to help the clergy; instead, the clergy will be there as resource people trained in theology to help the lay leaders in their theological understanding of the context of the society in which they work and live.

LOCAL CHURCH STRUCTURES IN RELATION TO THE LOCAL NEIGHBOURHOOD

In the future church the day-to-day life of the church would be expressed through many small groups or Christian cells within a work or social situation rather than through the weekly congregation in some large parish church. John Taylor in the article I have already quoted says:

> ... house groups or Christian cells or neighbourhood groups are the real growing edges of the church in the modern world, and they offer a milieu in which Christians could most vividly experience the therapeutic, interpretative and dynamic fellowship of the Body of Christ ... when Christians meet regularly in small groups with a minimum of traditional ceremony and professional leadership, they cease to be passive adherents of a folk religion and become articulate and capable of passing on their faith to others.[4]

154

Unfortunately the house-group movement has become linked with a certain type of fundamentalism and is often seen as an alternative church separating itself from other churches, rather like an exclusive sect. But this is a corruption of its true function. House groups are simply a recognition that, while in a village the local church is a natural focus for the community, in a large parish of many communities the natural gathering is not necessarily in the building of the church but in the many groups which form together through some common element – for example, the many different groupings (ethnic, different life-styles, professional and work groups) – such as I found in the parish of Camberwell. Members of these groups find the kind of strength and articulation of which John Taylor speaks more naturally at first through association with their own kind where they can experience support and openness with each other, make their own link between text and context in the articulation and propagation of the Gospel and also plan what responsible action is needed in the community. In this way each group develops the maximum potential fulfilment of its members and keeps a watchful eye on areas of injustice or exploitation. Each house group will probably also want to experience its own forms of worship and should be free to do so. From this much might be learnt by the whole church as to what is required of grass-roots worship rather than imposed worship.

As each house group would be functioning regularly, possibly meeting each week, there will be obviously times when the group not only prays together but wishes to celebrate communion together. In this case, since it would not only be impossible but undesirable for a priest who is not a member of the group to be brought in to preside, the whole question of lay presidency of the Eucharist at such house gatherings has to be seriously considered. This is to be seen, not as an alternative to ordained presidency as the norm, but as representative of the ordained ministry in the special setting of the situation. The president on such occasions would be the natural leader appointed by the group, who would be authorised by the local ordained ministry to fulfil this function. Out of this might also arise something that has already been experimented with in some dioceses, a local priesthood – that is, men (and, in due course, women) who have local knowledge and background offering themselves for training to come back and serve the local area within their natural milieu. The pattern would be very like that often exercised in the Greek Orthodox Church, where a local man is taken out of his village community, receives training in liturgy and doctrine and returns to his native place to work. There would be no question of such a local priest becoming generally available to serve anywhere in a diocese or rising to higher office in the church any more than there would be of a local village priest in the Orthodox Church becoming a bishop. This is not because the local priesthood is an inferior order of priesthood (there is no inferior order, only one priesthood) but because the whole point of a local ministry is that it is chosen for its local value, the value of someone whose knowledge and sensitivity to the area will give that extra to the work of the kingdom of God which arises from that background. Since it would not at all follow that such local gifts would equip someone to work in a totally different background, it would obviously be foolish to move him or her from the area. The Tiller Report summed up the situation:

> The differences between local and diocesan priest should be seen in terms of appointment, training and function, not in ordination. In view of the particular discernment of gifts leading to the ordination of local priests it is unlikely that many of them would be called to become diocesan priest ... before undertaking the work of a diocesan priest a local priest would clearly need to undergo further processes of selection and training but no further ordination. This would in no sense imply that the local priesthood is in some sense 'inferior'; further selection and training either is or should be the invariable rule when a priest transfers from one type of work to another.[5]

On the last sentence might be raised this query: if that is true, should not each step in the hierarchy of the church require further training as well as for those appointed to specialist ministry from parish ministry? – a question I will consider in the later chapter on training.

If then the normal community in an urban area is the local group, the normal ministry will obviously be also a local ministry. The report *Faith in the City* strongly supported local ministry for the following reasons:

(i) ' . . . it derives inevitably and naturally from what is meant by a fully local church which reflects the culture of its area. By this we mean an indigenous church, open to God, to each other, to the neighbourhood, to the world, and to understand the present and potential spirituality of the area.'

(ii) Local ministry in urban priority areas 'would be a strategic part of the task of reconciling the local church to the local community, particularly in the sense of encouraging a closer identity between the two'.

(iii) Local ministry 'must be seen as part of the recognition by the church that traditional ways alone will not enable it to meet its responsibility to local Christian communities in urban priority areas'.[6]

These recommendations were made in 1985, and it would be interesting to know how many areas have adopted the principle of local non-stipendiary ministry (I mean local as distinct from general NSM which is now fairly widespread). I have specific knowledge of only two – namely, at the Bethnal Green experiment in London diocese and the Brandon Scheme in Southwark diocese. In the diocese in which I now live there is no local ministry, although it would be invaluable for the staffing of many country villages as well as for some of the urban areas of the diocese.

THE INTERRELATIONSHIP OF LOCAL GROUPS, AREA CHURCH AND DIOCESE

There will be three aspects of these relationships:

(a) Local groups and area (parish) church

John Taylor highlights the situation of the local groups in relation to the parish church:

> ... it has a function, and a glorious one, as a cathedral gathering-place of the little congregations of which it should be made up. Their progress and their problems should be named there in the intercessions of the larger congregations and occasionally reported fully, so that other groups can be aware of them and all celebrate together the joy and vitality of the fellowship they experience at the smaller level.[7]

In urban areas there will probably be need of far fewer churches, since the previous parish boundaries will no longer apply. Instead of many churches ministering to a handful of people, as I saw all too often in the urban areas of south London, I would suggest retaining just a few of the more beautiful or well-planned churches to which members of the small groups could be brought by transport to form a large, celebratory congregation for the Sunday or festival occasion, for 'small groups need to be complemented by the glorious occasions and celebrations in the local parish church'.[8]

A group once worked out in the deanery of Camberwell, which had then ten parishes with ten churches most of which struggled with a very small congregation each Sunday, that the whole area could be better served by having many local groups and three churches, each having a somewhat different churchmanship but each offering either a glorious ancient building or a modern building with good rooms for other activities.

(b) Functions of the area church

The 'area church' (it would no longer be a parish church) could also provide a local headquarters team of diocesan clergy and laity from the various groups who, together with specialist clergy for particular work, would plan together the general policy for the area. It would be particularly valuable in a mixed local area – with difficulties of how to combine in true community people of mixed race, life-style, wealth and culture – to have a team of specialists, both clergy and laity, able to give help from their own skills and provide pastoral counselling and spiritual direction to the local group and the local priest. Such teamwork between the local and diocesan or area specialists could provide much greater opportunity of achieving some real influence for the kingdom of God than a lone parish priest struggling without any special understanding of the area and often simply overwhelmed by the weight of indifference and hostility surrounding him.

(c) Processes of decision-making

On the same principle, that decision-making in an area must be related to the needs of the community as a whole, the local church should always make it clear by its methods of functioning that it is more concerned with being outward-looking rather than inward-looking. At present this is seldom reflected in the agenda of the deanery and diocesan synods; much more time is given to matters of concern only to the church than to those of interest and concern to the locality. Recently an inordinate amount of time has been given in all synods to questions of the ordination of women, ecumenical co-operation and marriage after divorce. Although all these are important to the church, and to a certain extent to society, they are not of primary importance, especially in urban areas. When I was in Camberwell I often said that I could go into any pub any night of the week and be sure that people would not be discussing the ordination of women, the validity of Anglican orders or marriage in church after divorce – but they could very well be discussing sex or politics in relation to personal matters of relationship or justice! If we are to continue to have deanery and diocesan synods (although I would think it better to have regional synods covering the same regions as local councils and county councils or borough councils), then it must be more clearly shown that their agenda and decision-making are related to the actual concerns and needs of the area. This need is clearly recognised by the *Faith in the City* report:

> ... the church has to be ready to challenge any under-

standing of community which neglects the needs of its weaker members, which is concerned with individuals' rights and material possessions at the expense of the common good, or which is indifferent to the interests of those who happen to be outside. A Christian community is one that is open to, and responsible for, the whole of the society in which it is set and proclaims its care for the weak, its solidarity with all, and its values which lie beyond the mere satisfaction of material needs.[9]

The Report also emphasises concern for those who are alienated:

> ... it is only when the church itself is sensed to be a community in which all alienation caused by age, gender, race and class is decisively overcome that its mission can begin to be authentic among the millions who feel themselves alienated, not only from the church, but from society as a whole.[10]

The last point shows that the church has still a long way to go. A church which has very few blacks on its synods, which still spends time harassing homosexuals and which is largely middle-class and middle-aged, does not have much integrity in speaking to society on these alienations.

In all these various ways the concepts of a local church and ministry and of regional areas will help the formation of a different image of a grass-roots church working out its relationship to the neighbourhood and responsible action within it on a basis of equal authority and functioning rather than on a hierarchical basis. The local priest will not in any sense be above the laity, since both are from the same background and knowledge, nor will the laity be dependent upon him or her; some of the laity may well have more knowledge and better understanding of contextual theology than the priest. A relationship of interdependence rather than dependence will be formed which is far more in accord with the way God works in creation and the structure of his world. Still less will it be assumed that the bishop has more right to decree on his own personal initiative and viewpoint what is for the benefit of a whole diocese. The wise bishop will listen carefully to the many reports which will come to him from the regional synods and together with representatives from those regions decide on a basis of equality not superiority what in the whole diocese will contribute most to the extension of the kingdom of God.

1 Gerald Priestland, in the *Listener,* July 1982.
2 John Baker, *The Foolishness of God* (Darton, Longman and Todd 1990), p. 336.
3 Ruth Etchells, quoted in the Tiller Report, *A Strategy for the Church's Ministry,* General Synod 1983.
4 John V. Taylor, *A Church Reshaped* (CMS 1975), pp. 11, 13.
5 John Tiller, *A Strategy for the Church's Ministry,* p. 123.
6 Report of the Archbishop of Canterbury's Commission on Urban Priority Areas, *Faith in the City* (1985), pp. 113, 114.
7 John V. Taylor, op. cit.
8 *Faith in the City,* p. 137.
9 Ibid., p. 59.
10 Ibid., p. 60.

23

THE WIDER COMMUNITY OF CREATION

Changing structures and attitudes go beyond the life of the locality and the nation to the whole wider community of creation, now under more threat than for many generations. Moltmann emphasises both the threat and the community of all creation:

> There is a vicious circle of death which runs from human society to the natural environment and from the death of trees rebounds on human beings. The human creation of modern industrial society is leading to the exhaustion of nature.[1]

God's image on earth is not the solitary human being but true human community.

> It is not individual parts but the community of creation as a whole which reflects God's wisdom and beauty. Man has therefore no rights to act as an individual apart from consideration for the whole community of creation. The life of creation is the communicating community of creation.[2]

The interdependence of all life is now emphasised by many scientists, and conferences are constantly warning against the damage to the future of humanity resulting from small, short-term interests taking precedence over the realities of the future life of the planet. Sir Fred Hoyle, the British astrophysicist, says, 'Everything exists by courtesy of everything else', while Fritjof Capra has written:

Quantum theory reveals a basic oneness of the universe. It shows that we cannot decompose the world onto independently existing smaller units. As we penetrate into matter nature does not show us any isolated basic building blocks but rather appears as a complicated web of reactions between the various parts of the unified whole.[3]

Yet, despite the extreme urgency of the damage being done to the community of creation, there is little indication either in the national synods of the churches or in the life of the local church that high priority is given to this in theological thinking and practical action. In political life short-term expediency prevails over the long-term needs of human beings. In the life of the church the internal concerns and the limited loyalties of a sectarian group often prevail over the prophetic insight and proclamation of the kingdom of God. Ronald Preston speaks of the need to be constantly critical of existing structures and of the need to speak and act prophetically of the need for change, but he also recognises how often the larger canvas is ignored and obscured by domestic issues:

> In presenting the challenge of the kingdom of God Jesus created the core of a new community . . . its membership is in intention universal and transcending the social and political divisions which human beings create against one another . . . by contrast it is astonishing how faith inspired by the radical challenge of Jesus' parables and gnomic sayings should have so domesticated them in the course of Christian history and been so uncritical of whatever structures existed at the time.[4]

What then should the church do if it is to steer the world towards reconciliation of the created order with the purposes of God rather than follow short-term expediencies of market profitability? As throughout this book I shall apply to this question the same principles of reality and creativity. The reality is clear – again, to quote Moltmann: 'Nothing in reality exists of itself and rests in itself. All beings and entities with life exist and live with one another for one another and in one another in the wider context of the cosmos.'[5]

AREAS OF WORK FOR THE CHURCH

Creativity will be needed to gear all policies and thinking to the wider canvas of the unity of the cosmos. For the church there will be three areas of involvement: (1) self-examination and developing wider loyalties and understanding of Christian responsibility; (2) education, spreading understanding of the community of creation among church members; and (3) change of life-style to be consistent with ecological needs.

1. First the church needs to take a very critical look at itself. Sadly in the course of history the churches have been as guilty as any political or ethnic group of giving loyalty and support to limited concerns. One of the tragic facts in the course of history is that religion has been as destructive as it could be creative. We think of the past with its wars of religion, its Inquisition, its bigotries, persecutions and burnings, times when the teachings of Christ mattered less than power struggles and the dogmatic allegiances of one sect fighting another. Even today, in many areas, it is much the same. In Ireland the murderous violence between those 'thugs' who dignify themselves by the name of IRA and Loyalists are in neither case loyal to the Jesus they claim to support. But it has to be said that the sectarian violence between Protestant and Catholic has its roots in the segregation policies and dogmatism of the Roman Catholic Church and the more extreme Protestant churches in Ulster; for them the unity of the whole is less important than the calls of loyalty to the lesser.

This is equally true in other areas. The 'moral majority' in the USA had no hesitation in aligning itself with the most right-wing attitudes to nuclear might, justifying even nuclear war as being predestined by the doctrine of Armageddon. Most of the extreme forms of religion, such as the Moonies and some of the Jesus cults, have practised massive indoctrination, even in one notorious case to call for mass suicide in devotion to its leader. Adherents of Islam have justified murder, kidnap and hijacking by claiming devotion to the divine will. I mention all these sad facts of history past and present to show that it is very easy for religious devotion to be as blind to the ultimate unity of mankind as are the forces of race or economic greed.

So if the church is to help towards an attitude of mind which will put the community of the whole of creation as a first priority, then it must cease to place loyalty to sectional interests above loyalty to the reconciling power of Christ with all creation. 'All things are reconciled through him on earth or in heaven' (Colossians 1:20), and that means not only reconciliation of human beings within themselves, but also with each other and with the rights of animals, plants and the whole environment of the planet – the atmosphere, the seas, rivers and forests. Just as a human being unreconciled to his or her true self is a menace within society, and a divided society comprising unreconciled groupings is a force for destructive conflict, so the wholesale pollution of the earth – destruction of rain forests, acid rain, fouling of seas and rivers – means that humanity and the planet are at war with each other, and the loser in that battle can only be humanity. For Christ also said: 'I come not to bring peace but the sword' (Matthew 10:34), which surely means that if human beings choose to be loyal not to him and his reconciling love but to their own limited sectional interests, then as a fact, not desired but real, there will be destruction not peace.

It is a sad irony that the most destructive thing in human society is often not individual selfishness and aggressive tendencies but rather a distortion of the object of love and loyalty. The record of history shows that some of the worst destructions have been through unselfish loyalty and devotion to tribe, nation, religion or political ideology. The main trouble with human beings, especially male human beings, seems to be their excessive loyalty and devotion to some limited and narrow cause rather than to the benefit of humankind and the whole of creation. The number of victims of individual crimes is as nothing to the masses cheerfully sacrificed in blind devotion to what is thought to be the right cause, religious or political, in fanatical but mistaken loyalty to king and country, leader or group.

Bishop Butler in the eighteenth century is reported to have said: 'God preserve us from enthusiasm.' One can understand what he meant, when we see the disastrous effects of enthusiasm in Ireland and the Middle East at this time, but what he should have said was: 'God preserve us from enthusiasm for limited causes – God give us enthusiasm for the whole community of creation.' There is a world of difference between primitive identification with a cause or with limited business or political interests and mature forms of integration with the whole of society. Integration preserves the autonomy and responsibility of the individual in the social, political or ecological whole; identification with a narrowly defined group implies a surrender of both autonomy and responsibility, a surrender of both critical faculties and moral responsibility.

In all fields and especially in the ecological field the churches should be discouraging devotion to a group, whatever that group may be, and looking always to encouraging responsible understanding and support of the needs of the world and the planet as a whole. That is what is meant by 'love God and love your neighbour'. To love God is to love, not destroy, his creation, and to love one's neighbour is to see 'neighbour' as meaning not just family or the person next door, or the country, or one's own race, but all people everywhere: to see the Third World and its needs as important as the affluent North, the animal and its needs within the general purposes and good of all creation. Equally, to 'love myself' is not to destroy myself, which is what industrial expansion is doing, whether consciously or unconsciously.

2. The churches must consistently and thoroughly – in their preaching, teaching and study groups – see that each congregation fully understands the theology and ethics lying behind the community of creation. Basically this theology lies in the following:

(a) To accept God as creator means to see that all our

166

activities affecting people and the planet are creative rather than destructive.

(b) To accept God as incarnate and redeemer means to restore and recreate that which we have defaced or corrupted by our sin or greed, to turn from grasping and greed to the enjoyment of people, animals and nature for their own sakes. The dominion of humankind over all creation should not be a tyranny oppressing the earth for their own narrow interests.

Schumacher has spoken of modern science as a 'science of manipulation' rather than simply knowledge of God's creation. The mentality of scientific materialism which has looked upon nature as something to be exploited and used up for human convenience is still dominant. To quote Schumacher again: 'We are far too clever today to be able to survive without wisdom.'[6]

We have mastered nature but lacked wisdom. We would do well to remember the words in Proverbs: 'For the man who finds me [i.e. wisdom] finds life . . . all who hate me love death' (Proverbs 8:35–6 RSV).

We straddle the earth like bloated children, consuming its riches greedily and fouling it with our wastes. When we compare pre-modern civilisations with ours, they were more properly balanced according to the rhythms and balances of nature. Our present civilisation is programmed one-sidedly for development, growth expansion and conquest of nature rather than for co-operation with nature.

(c) To accept God as Holy Spirit means respect for all existence, which is upheld by his spirit and imbued with his energy. Again this is a co-operative rather than a competitive attitude to nature.

> A perception of the divine spirit in all things gives rise to a new view of the world; the mechanistic and atomistic picture of the world is replaced by a view of the world in terms of organism and energy. If the spirit of God is poured out on the whole creation, then the divine spirit creates the unity and the community of all creatures with one another and with God.[7]

167

(d) To accept our human nature as made in God's image and destined to grow towards unity with God means that use of the material is determined by the goals of the spiritual. It is our attitude to life, our sense of responsibility for our world and our acceptance of that responsibility which will affect the material and therefore our own struggle towards the ultimate perfection of being 'one with God'. As a result then of understanding ourselves we can develop a moral ecology which consists in, as Moltmann says, living one's life in agreement with the law and rhythms of the earth-system by which we all exist.

We can already see what happens when we pamper ourselves with every new 'gimmick' of a consumerist society and do not live according to the rhythms of nature: many modern diseases – thrombosis, heart attacks, obesity, ulcers – are the result of unnatural ways of living, which not only destroy our environment but also destroy ourselves.

Since all this is perhaps the most important theological and ethical issue of the day, why is not more heard of it in the churches? After one sermon I preached on the theme of ecology I received more congratulations than usual, and several members of the congregation said that they had never heard a sermon on ecology. Yet church members need to concern themselves with ecology as a major Christian issue. It is true that the Board for Social Responsibility has done some very valuable work on ecological issues but, as so often happens with matters dealt with by the General Synod, little of this seems to permeate through to local church members and form there the matter for serious study.

So the second task of the churches at this time is the task of education, not just at the top level but at all levels of church activity. If we are to realise my overall theme, that the text of the Gospel must always be related to the context of society, we cannot afford to be the quiescent, relatively ignorant people that we so often are. To hear many Christians talk one would think that Christianity is a simplistic matter of 'being good, nice to family and neighbours and above all respectable in matters of morality', but the problems of the environment are not subject to such simplistic solutions. We need to study the issues and then take action

168

as far as we can, but the action, as always, needs to be motivated by understanding of the issues. I would suggest the following educational programme for every church.

Study some publications from such groups as Friends of the Earth, the Ark, the International Institute of Environment and Development. A study of Moltmann's book, *Creating a Just Future*, could provide valuable background knowledge of the community of creation. If it is argued that these are only for the well-educated, I can assure you from experience that, like most matters of theology, they can be broken down into simpler language by study leaders who will take the trouble to distil the essential themes so that their groups can understand. Such material can also be regularly included in the parish magazine.

Then, in the light of such knowledge, we can learn what action we can take. There has been much evidence throughout Europe and in the events of the Soviet Union of the power of ordinary people like ourselves to affect issues. But nothing happens if we do not take action. We have a duty, according to our capacity, to write letters to the press or our member of parliament, to lobby and demonstrate and to support, by our votes, the local and national parties which show most concern about the environment, and we can keep an eye on what is happening in our own neighbourhood. All this should be encouraged and supported by local church authorities. Nothing is ever achieved by apathy and inaction; an ineffectual people, an ineffectual church, will in the long run lead to an ineffectual democracy, and that way lies tyranny. Creation and resurrection go together, but so assuredly do destruction and death.

3. But thirdly, as with most things in life, it all comes back to ourselves and our own styles of living. There must be changes in life-style if ecological issues are to be resolved. We cannot continue with excessive consumerism or tolerate a situation in which the poor of the Third World are compelled to cut down forests because the rich minorities in their countries will not allow them to live properly. The latter demands international action, perhaps of sanctions or

boycott of such rich 'vultures'; the former demands that Christians seriously consider a simpler life-style, not one of deprivation but of greater simplicity. The case for a simpler life-style has been set out clearly by Bishop John Taylor in *Enough is Enough* and Ronald Sider in *Rich Christians in an Age of Hunger*.[8]

For example, consumption of fossil fuel is linked closely to economic growth; the higher the standard of living, the more energy we use. Do we need all the cars we have? When I had a burglary in my last parish (by economic standards a rich one) someone said to me, 'Why don't you leave one of your cars in the drive each day?' – that household had five cars! Is more than one car really necessary to a household? Would it not be better if public transport were improved? Cannot Christians learn to share their cars more for shopping, for going to church and to social events? Other actions which can be encouraged in every parish are the recycling of paper, bottles and other materials. (How many forest trees are cut down to provide the mountains of paper sent out before every meeting of General Synod?)

We can also discourage unnecessary consumerist spending, especially at times like Christmas. It is possible to celebrate Christ's birth without giving ridiculously expensive presents and unnecessary Christmas cards – we can send these just to the old, the lonely and those we rarely see. Christians should have more incentives than most to be willing to spend that much more on buying the 'environmentally friendly' articles now stocked in most supermarkets and to pay the extra cost necessary if there is to be proper care of the environment over sources of heating and energy and purer water. There are so many small ways in which we can help to save the planet: for example, by joining one of the Green groups or organisations; wearing warmer clothes in winter so that we need less heating. All this needs encouragement and constant support from pulpit, press and parish magazine.

It is therefore right that this long section on community should end with the community of creation. The Christian church began with a small group living in community. In small groups community is developed personally; through the character of structures community is increased or diminished; what we do on this planet either creates or destroys community. In every sphere of life, therefore, community is of the highest importance. Remember: 'Human individuals develop in community and the human community changes.'[9]

In a world which has placed growth before society, centralisation before local community and profit before the care of the community of creation, perhaps the church's greatest task is to be continually creating and recreating community. If the church does not do this, it is highly questionable what useful purpose it is serving in society.

1 Jurgen Moltmann, *Creating a Just Future* (SCM Press 1989), p. 51.
2 Ibid., pp. 56, 67.
3 F. Capra, *The Tao of Physics*, quoted in 'Buddhist Physics', Schumacher Lecture 1979.
4 Ronald Preston, *The Future of Christian Ethics* (SCM Press 1987), pp. 174, 172.
5 Moltmann, op. cit., p. 58.
6 E.F. Schumacher, *A Guide for the Perplexed*, Jonathan Cape 1977.
7 Moltmann, op. cit., p. 57.
8 John V. Taylor, *Enough is Enough*, SCM Press 1975; Ronald Sider, *Rich Christians in an Age of Hunger*, Hodder 1978.
9 Ibid., pp. 9, 57.

24

REALISTIC TRAINING FOR CLERGY AND LAITY

I would now like to suggest ways by which training of both clergy and laity could be made to relate more realistically to the tasks which each have in the world. I will also indicate what I see as the relationship between the specific training of the clergy and that of the laity and what aspects of training can more suitably be done together rather than separately.

It will help us to understand the connection between clergy and laity if we realise that in the early days of the church the priesthood of Christ was shared by the whole Christian community. To be a priest was to share in the high calling of being a representative, to bring God to humanity and humanity to God – that is, to serve as a channel of communication between God and the world. That was the purpose of all who became Christians; the mission of the people of God is to be carried out by participation in Christ through baptism and belief. Peter called them to become 'a holy priesthood . . . a royal priesthood, a dedicated nation, and a people claimed by God for his own, to proclaim the triumphs of him who has called you out of darkness into his marvellous light' (1 Peter 2:4, 9 NEB).[1]

This priesthood was a very different concept from that of the old Jewish levitical priest; rather was it the whole church transforming human existence in community by opening up to the action of the Spirit and to a divinely given love. Of course any new community needed leadership, and Christ, in giving leadership through the twelve apostles (the number of the tribes of Israel), was making them symbolic of the whole people of God. This leadership was not by priest over people but the necessary leadership of those who for one reason or another were seen by him as right to preach the word, to feed his flock, to care for and love the sheep, to reconcile by absolution or to separate by divine judgement. Always the understanding was that leadership also demanded that the leader be a servant – to the poor, the oppressed, the enslaved, the unjustly treated, and the blind (in every sense). Even the judgement was a 'judgement on love by love' (Matthew, ch. 25).

This idea of leadership was continued and extended in the analogy which Paul makes frequently to the church as the Body of Christ. Within that body there are many members; each one has his or her own particular function and leadership qualities, again not on the basis of priest and laity but on the basis of the needs and resources of the whole body. The church moved far away from that idea as it developed a hierarchy of bishops and priests who embodied all the leadership functions and qualities and a laity who became servants of the clergy, rather than the reverse as Christ intended. As a result, training also became divided into separate training for clergy and laity and gradually less and less of the latter. When discussing the structures of the church, we saw their failure to meet present realities. So also is there a comparable failure of present methods of training.

It is no longer a matter of what training is suitable for clergy and what for laity, but what training is necessary for the functioning of the church as an agent of the kingdom of God in the context of the present day, and for the extension of that kingdom. Instead of a distinction in training between one for the priesthood and one for the laity, we should look at all the kinds of training needed in the modern church and then seek to find and train those who come forward and are selected for their suitability for whatever form of leadership is needed. The ordained priest or bishop may, and probably will, be a focal person in whatever community he or she represents, since there will always be a need for someone to represent any group or community. On the other hand some who exercise leadership may choose not to be ordained or consecrated, and some who are ordained may not be actual leaders. The division, and therefore the different kinds of training, will be not between those to be ordained and those not, but between those who are accepted for carrying out different functions within the Body.

Training will then relate to all the functions – theological education, conducting worship, meeting public and prophetic needs, various kinds of ministry, and administration – in which leadership is needed. Ordination will be much less important than leadership needs, and only in certain areas, probably of public liturgy, will ordination take priority. Had we thought along these lines rather than on the hierarchical clergy/laity axis, we might have saved ourselves a great deal of friction over the question of ordination of women; equality in leadership by women would have been the crucial point, not ordination.

To illustrate this, consider the respective functions given to deacon, priest and bishop in the Ordinal in the Alternative Service Book and how they overlap and are related to the leadership of the church as a community rather than to any clergy/laity division:

The deacon is to work with the members of the church in 'caring for the poor, the needy, the sick and all in trouble . . . to strengthen the faithful, to search out the careless and indifferent, and to preach the word of God'.

The priest is to be

> as servant and shepherd among the people to whom he is sent . . . to call his hearers to repentance, and in Christ's name to absolve and declare the forgiveness of sins . . . He must set the Good Shepherd always before him as the pattern of his calling, caring for the people committed to his charge, and joining with them in a common witness to the world.

The bishop is called to

> lead in serving and caring for the people of God and to work with them in oversight of the Church . . . to further the unity of the Church, to uphold its discipline,

and to guard its faith. He is to promote its mission throughout the world . . . He is to have a special care for the outcast and needy.

Notice the similarities in the functions of deacon, priest and bishop. Each is to be concerned with caring, with serving the poor, the sick and the outcast. Each is to work with the whole people of God in a mission of reconciliation, proclamation and prophetic caring action to the world. Each is to fulfil in different ways the function of both shepherd and servant. There is no suggestion of superiority or of any vital difference between the functioning of the ordained ministry and that of the laity, since each function mentioned of bishop, priest and deacon is also a function of the whole people of God. This means that in our future training the focus is not on whether it is for clergy or laity, but on what is best for the functioning of the church as an agent of the kingdom of God in regard to the present needs for the extension of that kingdom.

Looking then at training from that point of view, it can be seen that in the future life of the church training of clergy and laity will be needed in all the areas which we have been discussing.

1. TRAINING IN THEOLOGY

Training in the relationship of text to context in the study of the scriptures will be seen as a continuing joint process of learning and application by both clergy and laity. Those to be ordained will probably continue to receive a fuller background in biblical and doctrinal study. The *use* of that study will be the joint work of clergy and laity – the latter contributing particularly their greater and more technical understanding of the areas of work and culture in which text and context come together. Thus the clergy, after ordination, will be trained together with the laity so that they work out together the proclamation of the church's mission to the world and the way by which that mission is achieved. This has already been recommended in the *Faith in the City* report as a means by which those who are to work in urban priority areas should be trained, but it could be equally applicable to all areas of the church's work:

> There are other factors which again call into question the appropriateness of traditional theological teaching methods. Lay people are learning, not just about the Bible, but how to *use* the Bible to reflect their own experience. Young clergy must have the confidence and skill to help them in this. Working among cultures (ethnic or working-class) and religions that are strange to the ordinand's own background must be prepared for by a serious effort to look at the Christian religion from outside the traditional perspectives of academic theology.[2]

The method of much theology today (often taken from liberation theology) is to reflect on the human situation first and then to look at that situation in the light of the struggle for the kingdom of God – the liberation of the poor and oppressed – and make our commitment to it.

I have already spoken of the failing of present theological training in respect of communication. It is a failing that must be overcome if we are not to be restricted to communicating only with a highly literate and educated group. It is said, for example, that it is only the more educated who will be interested in joining study groups. If the term 'study group' is used, that may well be so, but if they are known to be groups which are meeting in order to thresh out the problems and opportunities within the area in order to resolve conflicts and to achieve a better standard of living, both materially and spiritually, in community (which is basically what much of the kingdom of God is about), then I think many people would be interested. But to arrange such groups means knowing the culture and patterns of thinking and language of different groups in the area and adapting ways of communication accordingly. This is not too difficult whatever one's background, if the following general rules are observed:

(a) Listen to the way people talk, what they talk about and how they express themselves.

(b) Be aware of the particular interests and problems of a neighbourhood.

(c) Neither talk down to people nor above their heads.

(d) Be aware that in some groups feelings and 'the heart' count more than the head. (In a group comprising people from Brixton and from a suburb in Surrey one of the former said, 'We *feel* things here, you *say* things there.')

(e) Find out what newspapers most people in the area read and then learn from their style and language some guidelines for communication.

In the different areas in which I have served I have found that it is not the essential content of the Gospel which has had to be changed but details such as the words used, length of sentences, illustrations, and especially to know the people.

In all this theological training I would see the clergy pre-ordination training as concerned mainly with the more detailed academic study of the background of the scriptures and the history of the church in the development of doctrine, ethics and worship, as indeed it is at present.

The training which would be equally for clergy and laity is that which relates the text of theology to the context of society in contemporary life, social and political questions, economic, sexual and environmental ethics, since all these are as much the concern of laity as of clergy. Here the knowledge of the context provided by the training and experience of the laity will need to be joined with the complementary, deeper theological research of the text which is the expertise of the clergy. One method of doing this would be to have in each diocese teams, made up equally of clergy and laity, responsible for the organisation of such training done in areas probably corresponding to the boundaries of the local Anglican deanery. This training could be at weekly evening sessions to which representatives of clergy and laity from each parish would come. From time to time there would also need to be residential weekend courses (such as now take place in business management) for more specific training in such matters as administration, leadership and communication skills. Study days and study packs could also be used. But the real importance would be in the shifting of emphasis from mainly clerical leadership to that of clergy *and* laity according to skills and with no superiority of clergy over laity: the preaching, editing of parish magazines, preparation of courses, study packs, etc. will be as much the work of laity as of clergy; if anything, probably the laity will have more to give because of their own involvement in secular life.

2. TRAINING FOR CONDUCT OF WORSHIP

As I have already made clear in chapter 22 when writing on house groups, it does not matter who leads the worship, priest or lay person. Usually the focal person in the administration of the sacraments will be an ordained person, but not always. What is important is that conducting worship is not just a matter of who 'takes the service' but who trains those who are to take part in the worship. It is not only absurd when all has to depend on the clergy; it is also a waste of resources. A group of lay people preparing others for baptism or confirmation will be able to speak from their knowledge of their own children, the difficulties of contact with secular schooling and work, the possibilities of relating text to context in the areas of family life, work and neighbourhood probably better than a priest. Also the need to have to explain the meaning of baptism and the commitments of confirmation to others will reinforce their own theological knowledge and commitment to mission. (I hope that infant baptism will eventually cease and baptism and confirmation become a joint act of commitment for service in Christian mission to the world, as was originally intended. If this is so, the importance of training by the laity, experienced in the knowledge of the responsibilities of life in the world will become even more necessary.)

Similarly, training for marriage is even more effectively done by lay people, especially if the priest happens to be a bachelor. An example of the form such training can take is given in chapter 18. It will, of course, be necessary for such a group of laity helping to train others for marriage to receive training themselves in the full understanding of marriage and how to train others, probably from some such group as Relate.

I hope also, if the church ever agrees to the blessing of committed homosexual and lesbian relationships, that those who wish to make vows of permanence and stability may themselves be trained in the understanding of the value and difficulties of such relationships from Christian 'gays' who have achieved some years of good and stable life together.

3. TRAINING TO MEET SOCIAL AND PROPHETIC NEEDS

In this field especially there will obviously be training on the basis of need and skills rather than on a distinction between ordained and lay. If there is to be realism in discovering what training will be necessary, each parish or area will have to make – as is recommended in the *Faith in the City* report – an audit, or analysis, of what is specifically needed in that area and also what resources are available and need to be developed by training. This will probably best be done on an ecumenical basis, since in assessing the needs of an area it is ridiculous to be acting separately as denominations, especially in view of the limited resources in skills and numbers of each denomination. In *Faith in the City* there is a comprehensive plan for the carrying out of such an analysis of an area, together with the relevant questions which need to be considered and answered. To quote from the Report:

> We recommend such an audit to be viewed not as another form to be filled in but as a means of enabling local churches to undertake in a fairly consistent way an outward-looking review of the needs of their area.[3]

I would strongly recommend such an audit not only for urban priority areas but also for suburban and country parishes, but it must be emphasised that both in town and country all the resources of all the local churches in the area will be needed if the audit is to be done efficiently, for unless it is so done the information will not be accurate or of much use.

Then having examined the needs and resources of the area it will next be necessary to make a comprehensive survey of the needs and resources of the local congregations and work out what training they will need:

(a) Survey of skills

What are the various skills of church members in the area – their work skills, their relationship to local associations and political affiliations, their personal qualities, their status and grouping? Who would relate more naturally to artisan or professional groups, or to ethnic or sex differentiation? Who has better understanding of artisan or middle-class potentialities and problems? This survey will determine whether a person is best engaged in the more public activities of the church in relation to the wider world (such as lobbying MPs and civic authorities, demonstrations, public speaking, media contacts, local trades associations or trade unions, management structures) or whether he or she is best engaged in a more one-to-one task of counselling or support.

(b) Training to meet the public and prophetic mission of the church

Those who are to be involved in the more public relating of the Gospel to complex work, sociological or political situations will need very careful training in the more prophetic side of theology. Both clergy and laity can make fools of themselves and depreciate the message of the Gospel if, in preaching, writing or public statements and actions, they simply show their ignorance of the actual situation and their own prejudices or class bias. This training will require an understanding of what is meant by the kingdom of God and also an understanding of the situation at any particular moment in which the text and the context have to be brought together. Careful analysis of the prophets of the Old Testament will show that they were as thorough in their understanding of the situation as of the will of God within that situation. Anyone, therefore, who is to speak or act for the church publicly, either in the media or in the synods or councils of church, state or industry, should be prepared to submit themselves to a fairly exhaustive training both in theology and in the area in which they are to represent the church. (I think that no one should be endorsed as a candidate for General Synod or speak on television or radio unless they are prepared to undergo such training.) In every parish those who seriously take their Christian relationship to work or into local civic action would benefit from the kind of study and sharing practised in the Woldingham Business and Professional Group described in chapter 7.

(c) Training in personal counselling

There will be only a limited number of people, whether clergy or lay, who are called to or have the qualities for this public prophetic ministry. Every human being, however, in the course of ordinary living will be fulfilling the role of counsellor or being counselled at some time. One who is officially recognised as engaged in pastoral care, as are the clergy or committed members of a Christian congregation, will be sought out for counselling and expected to be trained in that skill. But they may not have had such training, and much damage can be done when counselling is treated either as giving advice or, even worse, manipulating someone into accepting a particular way of thinking.

Counselling, like other skills, is something that can be learned and developed. In each area (corresponding to the size of a deanery synod) it should be expected that there will be a group of people who either volunteer or may be selected for training in counselling skills. This group will then be subsidised by the churches for courses of training with qualified training bodies, on the understanding that they will offer their services when required. Their names would then be circulated throughout the area, so that when someone needs counselling for a particular problem they will know to whom to go. Such counselling would, of course, be in strict confidence and could be of considerable benefit to both clergy and laity, many of whom find themselves in situations of stress and have no idea where they can go in trust and confidence for understanding and a listening ear.

Some volunteer counsellors may wish to develop not only general counselling skills but also to know how to counsel in particular areas of difficulty: for example, bereavement, dealing with long-term illness at home, sexual problems of marriage or homosexuality, AIDS, care and upbringing of children, violence either as victim or perpetrator, resolving conflicts, problems of different periods of life (teenage, middle age, old age), family or work situations. These and many others need particular knowledge, and courses, study days and conferences are provided by various agencies, including in most dioceses the diocesan council for pastoral care and counselling. What is surprising, and sad, is that although the needs are great and growing, there are still few willing to undergo such training and to receive the help of those who have been trained. The clergy in particular are often isolated by the defensive barriers they feel impelled to erect, owing to the false stereotype of pseudo-perfection often given to them!

Although there is no such thing as Christian counselling separated from other counselling, there is a Christian perspective on life, and it often gives additional assurance to Christians to feel that they can go to someone who is both a trained counsellor and has the same perspectives and values that they have – provided, of course, that such values are objectively those of Christ and not of some rigid sect which believes it has the monopoly of all truth and morality!

4. TRAINING FOR VARIOUS KINDS OF CLERICAL MINISTRY

The Church of England has been too wedded to the idea of one generalised training for all who are to be ordained, with a result that the average stipendiary priest is expected to be a kind of 'jack-of-all-trades' with gifts of preaching, pastoral care, administration and organisation. The Roman Catholic and Orthodox churches have avoided this. In the

Roman Catholic Church there is a clear distinction between the training required for the intellectual and spiritual leaders and a simpler training for the average parish priest. It is expected that the parish priest has primarily a liturgical and pastoral role; for the more sustained mission work requiring deeper thought and spirituality the monastic orders of Jesuits or Dominicans will be called in, and for social work the Franciscans and others; for these will have had much longer and more specialised training. Similarly in the Orthodox Church where, as I explained earlier, the parish priest is a local man given simple liturgical and pastoral skills; the deeper intellectual resources and policy direction are in the hands of the bishops who are expected to be of a very different background and spiritual discipline.

To a certain extent the Anglican Church is beginning to recognise different skills for different needs. As in the Roman Catholic Church the monastic orders are now increasingly used in mission and evangelism, but it is still too much expected that the average parish priest will be an all-purpose man skilled at everything – with the consequent disillusionment when this proves not to be so. Although, as I have said, much training of clergy will be done jointly with the laity, the following points must be noted regarding clergy training for specialist ministry, for non-stipendiary and local ministry, and for refresher courses.

(a) Specialist ministry

In every area there will be some who have opted for training in special skills: evangelism, preaching and education, group leadership, counselling and spiritual direction. They should live in the area and be closely in touch with local conditions and needs, and they would be recognised throughout the whole area as those to be called in for specific purposes. Others will need to be trained for specialist areas of mission, e.g. teaching and education, youth work, industrial and social mission. However, in no case should clergy go on doing the same specialist work divorced from local circumstances for too long. My experience leads me to think that a wise division between specialist work and everyday parish or local life brings new life and understanding into both areas.

(b) Training for non-stipendiary and local ministry

The work of non-stipendiary priests, engaged also in secular work, and of ordained ministers drawn from the local area and returning to it, needs to be considerably extended through a training geared less to academic learning but directed intensively to the relation of text to context: the context for the non-stipendiary minister being the area of secular work in which he or she is engaged; and for the local minister being how best from personal experience to extend the kingdom of God in their area. It is likely that there will be expansion of these two kinds of ministry at the expense of what is now called 'full-time' ministry (mistakenly, since all ministry is full-time). This will be no loss but rather gain to the church, since such ministers will not only be more in touch with the real needs of the laity but the laity themselves will be less dependent upon the parish priest and will exercise, with suitable training, greater responsibility for day-to-day pastoral needs.

(c) Refresher courses for renewal and new responsibilities

It should also be recognised that training never ends. At present most training relates to pre-ordination, and to post-ordination for a limited number of years. However, it is often in the middle years of ministry that many priests become 'stale' and need the stimulation of further intellectual, spiritual and pastoral training. Also, since many clergy continue to exercise their ministry well into retirement years, there is need for them to be prepared for the very different feelings of being no longer 'in charge', and how best to help others in retirement from one's own experience.

In the hierarchical ladder too, each step up should be preceded by training for the new responsibility: a new bishop to learn what pastoral shepherding really means, a new archdeacon to learn efficient but caring administration and a new dean to be taught both the dangers and opportunities of cathedrals in the life of the church.

TRAINING FOR ADMINISTRATION

As has already been said, the administration of the church is too power-centred in the higher echelons of the clergy. If the church is to speak prophetically of greater democracy and freedom then these qualities must be seen also in the church. True, we have in this century created a synodical structure, but that structure is still heavily dominated by the clergy, and in each diocese the opinions of the laity are heeded less than the opinions of the clergy and much less than the opinions of the bishop. Usually appointments and changes in a diocese will be made from above. This predominance of clergy and episcopal direction will continue as long as the laity are not fully trained to understand the theology, organisation and needs of the church on an equality with their clergy and bishop. To change this will mean much greater emphasis being put upon lay training and also a much greater willingness on the part of laity to undertake administrative responsibility. If that were to happen the church could work far more effectively, with power at a grassroots level reaching from below to above, rather than the reverse as at present.

Don Cupitt has an interesting plan that the officers representing the church at the synods should be specialist in various fields, such as theology, psychotherapy, in drama or other areas. I do not necessarily agree with his areas of specialisation, but he makes the important point that ' . . . there will be no career religious leaders with spiritual power and sacramental rank. There will be no rulers and no shepherds. All will be priests to each and each to all.'[4]

I do not believe that there should be 'no rulers and no shepherds', especially the latter; the important point is that the rulers shall be rulers by general consensus and election, and that they shall be accountable to those whom they represent. Then the shepherds would be truly shepherds and not just authority figures who can only be approached at times of crisis.

I feel very drawn to the pattern of future ministry put forward by Gerald Priestland:

185

If I were obliged to rough out a blue-print for the church of the future, I would start with the need for good popular theology, to affirm that God exists and what he is like, and upon this try to effect a renewal of religious education at all ages. Next, I would drag the laity deeper and deeper into ministry of all kinds, joining lay orders, popping in and out of monasteries, preaching, healing – celebrating irregular eucharists, too, I hope.[5]

1 See also Revelations 1:6 and 5:10.
2 *Faith in the City* report.
3 Ibid., Appendix A.
4 Don Cupitt, *Radicals and the Future of the Church* (SCM Press 1989), pp. 170–71.
5 Gerald Priestland, the *Listener*, 1 July 1982.

25

A FUTURE FOR WORSHIP

I indicated in chapter 13 some of the difficulties that face us in present-day worship. There appears to be no pattern of public worship that appeals to more than a comparatively small minority of people – even the most well-filled churches will on any occasion have only a minute proportion of the total population of the area. That raises a number of questions:

1. Is the whole exercise of worship a cultural activity that can be expected to interest only a limited number of people? Should it take its place with other cultural activities where it is recognised without any feeling of guilt or concern that only some will be interested?

2. If this is so, then does evangelism have little to do with persuading people to 'come to church', which is what many who belong to churches think is expected of them when they set out to evangelise?

3. Even if people are persuaded to 'come to church' does that necessarily mean that they have any conception of what worship truly means? For all that seems to concern many regular worshippers is personal preferences: 'The service must not last longer than an hour'; 'The hymns must be well known and have tunes I can sing'; 'The ritual must be high (or low) according to my upbringing'; 'Nothing must be said in the sermon to upset me'. There is more here of 'I' than of God, more of timing than transcendence.

4. Or is worship a natural activity for a human being, and the fact that it is not being practised indicate the failure of religious groups to know how to develop this natural activity?

If the ideal of worship is, as has often been said, the highest act of which human beings are capable – the mirror of the reality in which we perceive God, the world and ourselves at the deepest level, the supreme expression of all that we are and all that we know God to be (to use definitions often given of worship) – then why is the actual far removed from the ideal, so that on the one hand the majority have no inclination to worship and even the minority who do rarely think of it in these terms.

5. Even if we are trying to express the ideal, how in practice do we do it? It is very easy to use these glorious pictures of worship; it is much more difficult to see how to develop them in liturgical practice.

I shall not be able to give any final answers to these important questions. I only hope to be able to throw out some suggestions which could motivate our future attitudes and our practice of worship.

THE HUMAN NEED TO COME TOGETHER

Robin Green, in his book *Only Connect*, says:

> I have been fascinated for over twenty years by the connections between worship and human need. What does it mean for people to be drawn close to the love of God in worship? What is going on inside people as they worship God? What is happening as people engage in the Church's liturgy?[1]

There is a very important question to be asked if we are to meet the various groups of people: those outside liturgical worship, the occasional visitors and the regulars who yet seem to have very inadequate views of what they are doing – a question which covers all these groups. What is it that causes people to want to come together? Worship contains a desire to be together and that desire at least is shared by most people and could be the connecting link between the worshipper and the non-worshipper.

In the main we are dealing with three groups of people who have that connecting link:

1. The vast majority who, whether they intellectually believe in God or not, have no felt need to meet for liturgical worship but who nevertheless regularly come together either in large groups – for cultural purposes or sporting occasions such as theatre, concerts or football – or in smaller groups for the exchange of views on a variety of matters, including questions of local or national interest often leading to action for protest and reform.

2. A quite large group who feel the need to come together and take part in liturgical worship on special occasions of celebration or grief but, once these have been fulfilled, see no need to come together for worship on a regular basis.

3. Those who do count themselves regular worshippers but often show by their attitudes that they have little understanding of what brings them together.

I believe that worship is essential to Christian belief, is not an optional exercise but a natural activity of the human spirit. Peter Shaffer, in his play *Equus*, says: 'Without worship you shrink: it's as brutal as that.' But the one thing we have to recognise immediately is that the concept of worship cannot be considered simply as being within the four walls of a church or just as participation in some liturgical activity. Worship if it is to be real has to grow out of a felt need to come together.

Coming together in small groups

Charles Reich speaks of a sense of community which arose in the 1960s among young people and describes that grouping as a 'togetherness':

> 'Together' expresses the relationship among people who feel themselves to be members of the same species, who are related to each other and to all of nature by the underlying order of being. People are 'together' when they experience the same thing in the same way. They simply come together to share a feeling, a moment

189

or an experience . . . many of them believe that sharing creative work, sensitivity groups, political demonstrations and confrontations will produce a creativity far beyond the sum total of what they could produce as individuals.[2]

Unfortunately this sense of community of the 1960s did not last. Bishop John Taylor speaks similarly of Christian groups:

> . . . the units of the scattered church are not Christian individuals, but twos and threes gathered together to provide the 'one-another-ness' in which the Holy Spirit possesses them. And even in such tiny cells the corporateness is not an end in itself, but God's means of thrusting out into the life-stream of the world those who are 'in Christ in Ephesus' . . . To treat these smaller units of Christian presence as being truly the local church in all its fullness and responsibility means that we should expect their activities to include as completely as possible four different aspects of Christian life and witness, namely, reflection, service, worship and evangelism.[3]

I see the value of linking in thought these two kinds of grouping. In a parish or area I would try to discover those groups in the area which express the togetherness in creative thinking or the life-style of which Reich speaks or, if they did not exist, try to create them. Then, for the purposes of community as mentioned in chapter 21 and also for the gradual introduction of concepts of meaning arising from the projects or community concerns which brought them together, I would link the Christian groups with these other groups so that mutual understanding is shared. Out of this could well arise appropriate symbolism within which worship becomes real. For example, a group of people comprising both Christians and non-Christians might be meeting to discuss the needs of housing within the neighbourhood. Out of this are bound to arise ideas about the kind of housing which helps to mitigate loneliness and integrates the needs of young and old. Further development into the kind of activity which brings people to need to be together in housing and the kind of symbolism or liturgy which could shape this activity might result in a new understanding of the value of worship. As Robin Green says: 'Liturgy, which is the vehicle through which worship is expressed, creates an environment in which human beings confront these sides of themselves which under normal circumstances they dare not face.'[4]

It may have to be a different kind of liturgy from that expressed through the Book of Common Prayer or the Alternative Service Book. To take the example I have quoted, what started as a discussion on housing might develop into profound questioning about the difference between aloneness and loneliness, and about the contributions which both old and young contribute to life and wisdom. This could lead to reflection on whether the experiences of aloneness and age are entirely material or whether there is a spiritual depth and, if so, how that can be expressed in a 'togetherness' symbolism and ritual.

In order that those who are Christians may contribute to such groups their own depth of spirituality arising from their beliefs, they should meet regularly in the small units of which Taylor speaks. The expression of Word and sacrament would be within their group meetings, probably on a weekday rather than a Sunday. Their ministry of the Word would be the discerning of the holy in the midst of the secular, the holiness of everyday living of which Martin Buber speaks:

> One should hallow all one does in one's natural life . . . one eats in holiness, and the table becomes an altar. One works in holiness and he raises up the sparks which hide themselves in all tools. One walks in holiness across the fields, and the soft songs of all herbs, which they voice to God, enter into the song of our soul.[5]

In the groups, in silence and discussion together, the contemporary situation would be brought under the searchlight of the Word, so that the presence of Christ could be seen to be in the work, neighbourhood and personal situations faced by the group. Ways would be explored by which the kingdom of God could be built locally in association with other groups. Members of the group would come to

191

see themselves as the little church offering themselves in the world for the Holy Spirit to work through them. The change would be that the group would no longer see itself as a pressurising and persuading group trying to draw others into the church, but rather as the church drawing itself into association with others in a 'togetherness' of search for meaning and action within the world.

If the group also found itself – as it would – expressing its 'togetherness' in a feeling of shared community of feelings as well as of thinking and action, then ritual or body actions would result from such shared feelings. But these would be real only if the people in such a group were free to be themselves in both their goodness and their badness. As Monica Furlong says, church congregations so often play at 'happy families', mistaking a papering-over of the cracks with Christian wallpaper as Christian love. Real Christian love is when badness can also be exposed: the resentments, jealousies, hatreds (even hatred of God) can be shared together to find healing and acceptance within the love of Christ.

The difficulty is that such expression can be made real only within a small community which has learnt to speak and feel the truth in love. Ritual actions such as the kiss of peace, when expressed in the public worship of a large church congregation, very soon become devoid of all meaning (I can understand why many people dislike the ritual hand-shake in the middle of the Eucharist, because so often it means nothing at all). On the other hand, when in a small group someone feels free to cry and the others gather round with a hug, these become ritual actions of a caring and loving community. Or when someone feels free to curse God or explode upon another member in rage and pent-up feeling, that becomes a ritual action of a free and open community finding healing and acceptance within the security of the love of Christ. In other words, if worship is not to be simply a matter of formalised words and actions but to arise out of a reality of reflection and emotion, then we cannot confine our understanding of worship to what goes on in a large building on Sundays; that kind of worship must be for other purposes, to which I shall come later. 'Small is beautiful' must also be true of any real contact with those who have not known worship and, as Robin Green says, of 'any attempt to make liturgy respond to an environment of meaning and belonging'.

As a result of this finding of meaning and redemption through silence, thinking together, relating text to context and an openness of expression of feeling and love, it is likely that the small group will want to express symbolically its feeling of community in Holy Communion. When this happens it would be ridiculous to have to go off to find a priest. The natural president of such an occasion would either be the host or the leader of the group, who would focalise in ritual what the group had been doing and feeling. The tramlines of sex, whether male or female, and canonical rulings would be wholly irrelevant. When Jesus used the ritual of the Passover to express a different meaning of a community about to be born out of love, grief, betrayal, anger and sacrifice, he had none of the ordained authority of rabbi or temple priest, but he was unquestionably the natural leader of that group on that occasion. He would have seen no conflict between what he did and the normal ritual authority of the priest in the temple. Neither is there today; for the large occasions of celebratory worship in the parish church there needs to be an ordering of function but, as occasions vary, so does the appropriate person to lead the functioning.

Coming together in large groups for particular occasions

The second of the three groups I listed earlier in this chapter, those who use the Christian ritual for particular occasions, are people who at various times in life want to come together to express their feelings symbolically but do not see any need to do this outside the particular occasion which has brought them together. Such occasions are when joy is to be expressed for the birth of a child, when two people are coming together to share life in marriage, or when grief brings people together to mourn at funerals. There may also be particular seasons of the year when the mood is of celebration, such as harvest-time, Christmas, spring, or occasions of national celebration – a royal jubilee or a thanksgiving after a time of crisis, such as war, or for relief from disaster – or again when the mood is one of grief at the death of a monarch, a great statesman or other famous member of society. On all these occasions and many others it has to be remembered that the main purpose in the minds of those who come together is to express feeling – joy or sorrow – not to be concerned with doctrine or the theological rulings of the church. If we do not realise and accept that and build on from there, we shall go on making cheap remarks about 'folk religion' and trying to impose rules which have no meaning or relevance to those who come to us. The result will be still greater separation between worship and life.

What has been critically called 'folk religion' is in fact much more in line with the concepts of the Middle Ages. Then the church had a clearly defined place in social life: church worship was a kind of public cultus in which the aims of society and those of the church were closely connected. The human ends of society were raised to the place of the divine and the divine stooped to give blessing to the human. Hence the close association of bishop and statesman, of festival and holiday, of saints and localities, of craft guilds and work associated with worship, of drama, art, architecture and music, all finding their subject matter in religion. Worship was in a real sense *public* worship, the worship of society, 'folk' worship in fact.

A society which lacks an overall philosophy of life and whose symbols have become technological rather than religious will lack communal cultus.

But people still feel the need to come together at times of joy or grief, or at times of great local or national rejoicing or crisis. They experience at these times a sense of what might be called 'the beyond in our midst', 'a depth of life', 'a sense of God', even though that God and that sense could not be sharply defined or even consciously recognised. Moltmann comes near to expressing the feelings of those whose worship is expressed in folk religion when he says:

When we cease using God as 'helper in need', 'stop-gap' and 'problem solver' we are, according to Augustine, finally free for the joy of God and the enjoyment of each other in God. Purpose-free rejoicing in God may then take the place of the uses and abuses of God. When theology is no longer necessary to practise philanthropy it certainly will not have to disappear, but it may then finally be done for God's own sake and out of infinite rejoicing in God which is in keeping with its true nature. Being there for others has its end to be with others in liberty. Being there for others is the way to the redemption of life. Being there with others is the form which the liberated and redeemed life has taken.[6]

In other words, the daily action of the church in the world is to be there for others, but its action in its worship is the spontaneous joy and hope of those who are liberated to be with others either simply rejoicing together or, in grief and crisis, supporting together with a sense of that which is beyond and yet incarnate – the crucified God with them in their suffering. Don Cupitt expresses the feeling of many who linger on the fringe of the church's worship and yet wish at times to be involved in what he calls 'discipline of the void':

I am advocating a religion of life in the sense of a spiritual discipline that enables us to accept and say Yes to our life as it is, baseless, brief, pointless and utterly contingent and yet in its very nihility beautiful, ethically demanding, solemn and final . . . we find eternal joy in emptiness, we say an everlasting Yes to the flux. That is our worship.[7]

But folk religion goes beyond the feelings of Cupitt in a way he does not wish to recognise – namely, that there is a sense of more than saying Yes to life as it is. There is also a feeling, albeit indefinable, that there is an Other who is there in joy and in sorrow.

So I am not at all scornful of the folk religionists who come to baptisms, funerals, weddings, midnight mass at Christmas, harvest thanksgivings, national jubilees and so on. Those who would wish to exclude all who do not come regularly to worship, from having their child baptised or who forbid a marriage service to those who have failed in their first marriage, are failing to recognise a togetherness, a desire to be with others in joy and in sorrow which is not far from the kingdom of God and is a salutary breaking out from that narrow individualism which in recent years has done so much to damage the sense of human solidarity.

Let us then welcome all who desire to come together with others in the symbolism of worship to express their deepest needs. By all means let us build upon that by using the occasion to build up greater depth: for example, by training for marriage (as outlined in chapter 18) or by encouraging a greater understanding of the meaning of death and its acceptance. The harvest festival will stress the interdependence of all creation in ecology, care for the environment and just distribution. If Remembrance Sunday is continued, let it be on 6 August, the day the first atom bomb fell, and be an occasion to speak of peace and the folly and crime of war.

I would also encourage many more such occasions for coming together to express our deepest feelings about life. Recently I experienced an example of this sort of worship. A man who lived in this area, and who was a county councillor deeply involved in local politics, came to see me. He said, with great courage and calmness, that he faced a very serious operation which could result in either recovery or death. He was not an orthodox believer, but he felt that if he died both his family and the community would expect some form of public memorial in the local church, and he would like me to take this and give the address. He drew up the memorial service himself, which consisted of a selection of music and poems expressing his own feelings about life and death. He came through the operation but shortly afterwards developed secondaries and died. The memorial, as he had prepared it, was used and I expressed what his life had meant in quality and involvement and the courage to face death. The service took place in a packed church and everyone said it was for them a very real experience of communal solidarity and understanding of the depths of life and death. Here was expressed, better than in any liturgical service, the value of a folk religion at a level which spoke with meaning and value to all present.

I often also think of those occasions in and after the war when people came out of their normal reticence and aloofness to express their shared risks in living and their common joy and thankfulness for the ending of war. The street parties and the local solidarity in times of need became liturgies of loving of a kind rarely experienced in life, even in the normal activities of churches. Paul Tillich sums up what worship can mean when, for a while, we stop living on the surface and get down to what is real:

> Eternal joy is the end of the ways of God . . . But eternal joy is not to be reached by living on the surface. It is rather attained by breaking through the surface, by penetrating the deep things of ourselves, of our world and of God. The moment in which we reach the last depth of our lives is the moment in which we can experience the joy that has eternity within it, the hope that cannot be destroyed, and the truth on which life and death are built. For in the depth is truth; and in the depth is hope; and in the depth is joy.[8]

THE QUALITY AND MEANING OF REGULAR LITURGICAL WORSHIP

In this chapter so far I have been concerned with the means by which we may bridge the gap between the insider and the outsider in church worship. Now if the outsider wants to become an insider, what has he or she the right to expect? Is there any function which is not being fulfilled by the local Christian group? Bishop Taylor holds that

> . . . it is the 'little congregations' which must become normative if the church is to respond to the Spirit's movements in the life of the world . . . a simple sharing of the loaf and the cup should be a natural summing up of the group experience . . . This is what must come

as the normal way in which the majority of Christians make the Holy Communion central to their lives.

What then is left for the weekly liturgical action of the parish church? Bishop Taylor simply says that 'the parish church may have an important function as a cathedral gathering-place of the varied smaller units lest they become in-group'.[9]

But there is more to it than that. Whatever future we may see for worship, there is no future in which all our parish churches will be closed down and no longer used for purposes of worship. There will be less of them, and in many areas the folly of maintaining a building which caters for about two dozen people once a week just because it is an ancient building will have been recognised, but there will still be churches, covering wider areas, where what we call public worship will take place.

What then will be the functions of worship in churches? First, the liturgy of the Word as expressing not so much the reflection and relationship of text to context – that will be taking place in the small groups – but rather the *proclamation and prophecy* which is more fittingly the task of public preaching; secondly, the sense of *celebration* of a worship which is meant to proclaim resurrection and new life; thirdly, the expression of that *transcendence* by which the sacramental offering of the outward and visible symbols is really seen and experienced as inward and spiritual, and the bread and wine of daily life is actually experienced as the presence of Christ. Public worship must express proclamation and prophecy, celebration and resurrection, offering and transcendence, if it is to be seen as separate from the worship in the small group or the worship expressing a particular need and yet related to and fulfilling both of these. Just as in other fields there is a difference between the dynamic functions of a small group and of a large group, so there is in the church; public worship is the dynamism of the large group.

What then can and should be done under the three headings I have mentioned?

(a) Proclamation and prophecy

Since this is usually the function of the leader of public worship it is one which particularly concerns the clergy. After many years of ministry I would echo the words of Robin Green: 'Why, I kept on asking, are sermons so badly prepared, when numerous lay people tell me that they are longing for connections to be made between their life experience and biblical tradition?'[10]

The function of the sermon is that of proclamation and prophecy, and every sermon should help the lay person to see how these dual functions can be exercised in the world. What is the proclamation? It is given directly to us by Christ himself: 'He has sent me to bring good news to the poor, to proclaim liberty to captives and to the blind new sight, to set the downtrodden free, to proclaim the year of the Lord's favour' (Luke 4:18–19). It is the preacher's task to interpret, in terms of the life experience of his congregation, who are the poor within the area and the nature of the poverty within themselves; who are the captives of ignorance, prejudice, intolerance and addictions that need release; what new sight and new vision is needed; who are the downtrodden, the outcast, the excluded who need freedom; and what building of the kingdom of God in the area is needed if the future is to be 'the year of the Lord's favour'.

Proclamation inevitably involves prophecy, and prophecy involves protest against all the forces within our society which cause poverty, oppression, alienation and exclusion. It is therefore ridiculous to suggest that religion and politics should be kept apart in the pulpit. Indeed, our preaching should be dealing with what liberation theology means in terms of our own society. It may not be the same as in Latin America, but unless liberation theology is worked out in the contemporary situation it is no true theology, for Christ is liberation and if we are not preaching both the personal and the corporate liberation of human beings we are not proclaiming Christ. As Kenneth Leech so rightly says:

> ... alienation, dehumanisation, oppression are political and personal realities and political and personal are

interlocked . . . If theology is not a theology of liberation
it is bound to be a theology of oppression. It cannot be
neutral, a theology of nothing.[11]

The preacher who is truly exercising his or her function
will first examine very carefully, with research into its own
background through reliable commentaries, what is the particular aspect of Christian proclamation contained in the
readings for the day. (The Alternative Service Book is more
helpful in this respect than the Book of Common Prayer, as
each Sunday and major day has a theme clearly worked out
in the Old Testament, Epistle and Gospel readings.) Then
the preacher will reflect, preferably with the help of thinking
or an audit done by local groups during preceding weeks,
what these readings are saying to the needs and 'liberations'
required in both national and local society. It will then be
the task of the local groups to relate text to context by
seeing the action which needs to be taken to carry the
proclamation forward into the details of organisation. If
the sermon has been typed out a few days beforehand, the
script can then be available to the groups and to anyone
who requires it for further study.

(b) Celebration and resurrection

If Christianity is to reflect the words of Christ, 'I am come
that they might have life and that they might have it more
abundantly' (John 10:10), then for public worship to have
any attraction it must express the sense of life abundance,
of celebration, of resurrection and new life. Many young
people say they find church worship boring. That is a great
condemnation of the way we do things, and there can be
no excuse if we present a faith of life abundance in terms
of dreary music, badly performed ceremonial, little colour,
poor reading and a general air of stifling conventionality.
Was it not Nietzsche who said: 'I could believe more in their
Saviour if they looked a bit more saved.' If worship is to
speak to human beings, it must express the contrasts and
feelings of human living. It must speak to life abundance in
all its moods – life triumphant and celebrative, life calm and

peaceful but not necessarily dull, and life in sadness in which there is nevertheless hope.

Worship must always be seen as a 'happening', not just a word-package. A happening involves every part of us – body, mind and spirit. I would like to see the Christian year reflected in ceremonial, but not just a ceremonial showing through the season whether a church is designated 'high' or 'low' by the way it does things. I hope that there will come a time when churches are neither high nor low but all are places where worship reflects the passions and feelings of life. To give an illustration: let the seasons of solemnity and preparation, such as Advent and Lent, be reflected in both music and colour and the use of liturgical dance together with the preaching, so that all that is done or worn or used speaks to the understanding that in Christian life there is sadness, but never despair; feelings of loneliness and understanding of the need to be a community towards the suffering, but never loss of hope. Let the restraint we show in our worship be reflected in our life.

Let us prepare for Christmas as we would prepare for an expected child – with that hope, tenderness and love which will extend into sensitivity and true care without possessiveness for our own children, and into concern for the children of the poor which shows itself in action – so that the present we buy is for those in need and not for those already having plenty. Let our preparation for Christmas speak both in worship and in life for the restraint which will do no damage to our planet by excessive consumption and will also remind us that in practical terms we are to care for the poor and the lonely and that 'in the evening of life we shall be judged by love on love'. A worship which can express that in symbolism and in practical action and thought should have something to say to the outside world of what life abundance means in terms of restraint for ourselves and care for others. And, as we do not celebrate the birth of a child until the child actually arrives, let us keep our parties until the Child is born, until Christmas. We often spoil the true feelings of celebration by doing all our celebrating before and during the two days of Christmas and Boxing Day, and then the rest of the twelve days are completely forgotten.

In the same way, and on an even deeper level, let Lent be a time of preparing for death – not in a morbid or dismal sense but rather in that symbolised by the deepest joy which knows that while worship and life must face crucifixion, behind the cross for ever now is resurrection. If eternal living means, as John Robinson said, quality of life, then Lent is a time when in worship all symbolism and ceremonial and music and dance should seek to show quality of life. It is a time of sacrifice, of real giving, abundant giving of both time and money for the sake of others, particularly for the sake of those who face death or terminal illness. Not only shall we dress our churches more soberly; that same sobriety will be reflected in our lives, in our own dress, our own discipline regarding food and drink, our own quality of life. Our worship will prepare us for the abundant living of true dying through the music of the great requiems or of parts of Elgar's *Dream of Gerontius*, through the restraint and yet the beauty of a dignified absence of colour of flower and vesture in the church (perhaps a simple cassock for all the leaders of worship), and also through the constant theme of finding new life *through* death not by the *avoidance* of death. Never will our worship show death to be the end: even when we face the cross on Good Friday we shall know, as the disciples on that first Good Friday did not know, that

Only when you have drunk from the river of silence shall you indeed sing.
And when you have reached the mountain top, then you shall begin to climb.
And when the earth shall claim your limbs, then shall you truly dance.[12]

Continuing with the idea that worship shall express the rhythms of life and feeling, let the great festivals of Christmas and Easter reflect the sheer uninhibited enjoyment of the celebratory event, the sense of party and conviviality. We are at Christmas shouting to the whole world: 'A child is born, but what a child!' God becomes one with humanity – Mary and Jesus bringing together for ever the unity of the female and the male in ourselves and the unity in the mind of God. And at Easter: 'Christ is risen. Christ is risen indeed, alleluia! Through death to new life, all things shout glory.' The appropriate response is then to let it all out! Let everything used in celebration *be* used: the rich colours in vestments and drapings; the most glorious and triumphant music; the processions, the trumpets, the incense and bells. And let us not forget also that the body joins in the sense of joy: the kiss of peace becomes a real hug of warmth and love, the liturgical dance is a movement of abandonment reflecting joy. The value of the charismatic movement has been that it has taught us to use our bodies in acclamation and prayer. (It might be a good idea to introduce into our worship clapping as a sense of appreciation or refusal to clap as a sign of disapproval – the good sermon or rendering of music to be treated with appreciation, the poor in preaching or music with silence. That might be very salutary for some of our preachers!)

Then there will be the seasons which might reflect the feelings of ordinary life – the period of the Sundays after Pentecost, for example. If worship is to reflect the feelings of life, then life is like that – there are times of sombre preparation and grief, times of great rejoicing and times when life is between the two, neither ecstatic nor sad. So again our worship must reflect and symbolise those ordinary times in a more restrained but not sombre ceremonial, in greater reflection by word and prayer on the daily themes of 'ordinary' life: Christ walking on the roads of Galilee or encountering people in the street and at the temple in Jerusalem, as we ourselves walk on the roads of life and work and make our daily encounters with their problems and joys.

(c) Offering and transcendence

In all our normal liturgical worship we have to be able to show clearly, on the one hand, the reality of daily life and of our emotions and feelings as we face its sorrows and its joys and its day-to-day decisions and, on the other hand, the sense of transcendence that there is more to life than the here and now, and that the presence of Christ is the presence and strength of the divine in the human. Transcendence is very difficult to communicate in worship, partly because while we are conscious that there is mystery in life which cannot be contained within the world of fact (our modern technological society), we are not sure what that mystery is and how we can express it to others. When Jesus first spoke of the mystery of the sacramental presence, 'This is my Body; this is my Blood', I am sure the disciples had no idea what he meant, but later, reinforced by their experience of the risen presence of Jesus, they were conscious of a strength and a presence standing with them against all difficulties and even death itself, which they could feel but probably could not articulate. It was this sense they had which communicated itself to others and made worship real.

When St Augustine said to his communicants, 'You are the Body of Christ: you are to be taken, broken, and distributed that you may be the means of grace and vehicles of the eternal charity to the world,' he was in fact laying down the principle which lies behind all life and all action. We and all our life, work, politics, home and personal relationships, are taken and offered at the altar in all their poverty as well as their goodness. It is only when we have seen what it is we are presenting to God that we can then reoffer ourselves to be consecrated: this is the fashioning of God's new world out of the old, the renewing and consecrating of our daily life that it may be broken, then rise again renewed by a presence greater than ourselves to enter into the world again during the following week.

It may not be of any great value to the average person to say, as Don Cupitt does, 'We find eternal joy in emptiness, we say an everlasting Yes to the flux. That is our worship.'[13] Yet it is the consciousness of the emptiness and of something behind the emptiness, the offering and of something behind and making good the offering, that spells out to most of us what is meant by transcendence. The sense of emptiness and yet presence is made very real in the poems of R. S. Thomas; I quote from one of them:

> He is a religious man.
> How often I have heard him say,

204

> looking around him with his worried eyes
>   at the emptiness: There must be something.
>
> It is the same at night, when,
>   rising from his fused prayers,
> he faces the illuminated city
>   above him: All that brightness, he thinks,
>
> and nobody there! I am nothing
>   religious. All I have is a piece
> of the universal mind that reflects
>   infinite darkness between points of light.[14]

Somehow, if we are to express transcendence we have to incorporate both of these feelings – the mystery of the unknown behind the uncertainty and the paradox of a conviction that is actually felt and expressed in the intercessions, in the offering of bread and wine. If transcendence is to mean both the mystery of reverential agnosticism and of conscious affirmation of belief behind living, then perhaps the fault in much of our worship is that we do neither. The mystery of doubt is not allowed to be there; the mystery of affirmation is just not there. James Joyce describes in terrible terms a Jesuit priest whose worship has left no mark on his life:

> His very body had grown old in the service of the Lord ... and yet he had remained ungraced by aught of saintly beauty. Nay, his very soul had waxed old in that service without growing towards light and beauty or spreading abroad the sweet odour of her sanctity.[15]

We have in all honesty to recognise that this is true of many priests and lay people. Many of those who have spent their lives within the shadow of religion and week by week have 'gone to church' have communicated nothing of the presence of Christ in their daily lives, or of conviction of a reality that reveals, in the bread and wine of daily life, the presence of Jesus in the offices, factories, homes and leisure activities of life. Samuel Miller puts it very strongly when he

205

says that it is possible to live within the church but, like Joyce's Jesuit, to go out from the church ungraced:

> ... it is to do all the things that religion requires of us, to live up to its rules and regulations and yet not to receive the fruits of it ... it is to know all the drudgery of church work and yet never to find the grace and glory of God working through it ... to bear within oneself all the pain and perplexity of life and then to cover them up with external activities and superficial considerations.[16]

So how is the transcendence of uncertainty and seeking and of the reality of life brought into worship to be communicated? One way would be through a much greater use of what is sometimes called 'testimony', but without the awful implications of piety and superiority, of fundamentalist dogmatism and a kind of judgementalism which often goes with the word when associated with evangelistic worship. What I want is for people to be able at points in the public worship to speak out of the realities of their life and problems, so that what has been threshed out in detail in the small group, as to how their beliefs have helped the resolution of difficulties, may be communicated briefly as a public offering. It could probably best be done when the offertory is brought up: the one bearing the bread to bring problems of home and work, and the other bearing the wine to bring the joys and sorrows which the symbolism of wine represents – each briefly but without inhibition. The other side of transcendence could be articulated during the intercessions – the mystery behind emptiness, grief and questioning which suffering and death brings, again briefly illustrated from the personal experience of the intercessor. Perhaps some poems, such as those by R. S. Thomas and some by Dylan Thomas, could be used together with passages from T. S. Eliot's poetry. If worship is the reality of divine depth in life, then transcendence will speak through intercession from the depth of our anguish to see if God is there.

What is said at the times of offering and intercession will be followed by some time of real silence, for silence also communicates transcendence in a way which a church

206

busied with 'talkative' and frenziedly active Christianity can never do. I find it strange that so little use is made of silence in worship, and that little preparation on the theme of the readings for the day is made by the small groups meeting during the week. Surely, if public worship is to be real, there needs to be a group in the parish whose function it is to study the theme for the coming Sunday, relate text to context by deciding together what that theme is saying to their own lives and area in anticipation of the proclamation which will be publicly made by the preacher. Then, after the Epistle and Gospel readings, the leader of the study group could make a brief two-or-three-minute statement arising from the group's thinking. The membership of such a group (it might be called the 'parish liturgical group') would, of course, be changed after a few weeks so that preparation for the theme of the coming Sunday could be shared through the whole congregation.

As to the use of silence, why are we so afraid of it? I would suggest that in every public act of Eucharist there should be a time for reflection on the readings and the sermon. Again, to have before the act of communion a period of silence in which we could individually experience and pray for the presence of Christ in the coming week – the Body and Blood in the bread and wine – would contribute greatly to the sense of transcendence.

I hope that I have shown how connecting links may be made between worship and the three groups of potential worshippers I identified earlier in this chapter, so that worship may come to be regarded neither as a bore nor as simply an occupation for a minority of strange people who 'like that sort of thing'. To summarise the links would be as follows:

(a) The mingling of the Christian groups with other groups in the area who come together for the facing of human and local problems so that into the thinking may be woven questions of value and meaning – the material and the spiritual united as naturally they should be. Out of this mutual coming together there could easily arise symbolic representations of communal sharing from which could be born, often without conscious recognition at first, a liturgy of a communal worship wherever people naturally meet. After all, that was how primitive liturgy was born in the early days of Christianity.

(b) The welcoming rather than despising of 'folk' religion as enjoyment of each other in God or as grief-sharing with each other in God. Such large-group sharing of particular occasions or seasons would strive to be as realistic as possible in the understanding of how people are thinking and feeling, and hope to build upon that to a deeper concern with the values of life so that such occasions would become no longer occasional but regular opportunities for coming together in that Holy Communion which John Robinson describes as being born out of holy community.

However, I think we should be very suspicious of the over-emphasis placed at present on so-called 'family' worship. This tends to preclude the large numbers of people – widows, spinsters, bachelors, 'gays' and lesbians – who are not within the conventional sphere of family life and supports the romantic picture often given of family life which bears no relationship to the reality. As Robin Green points out: 'There is a massive collusion in Western society against honest talking about the ambiguity of parenthood. The truth is that in many families, mothers and fathers slide down the razor-blade edge between violence and love.'[17] In the light of the need to bring reality to our worship let such days as Mothering Sunday and so-called 'family services' be occasions when real help is given by providing sympathetic but not idealised concepts of the difficulties as well as the joys of family life. Let it also be made clear that, for the church, 'family' means not the nuclear, secular family but the 'family of God' which includes, not excludes, the many 'singles' already mentioned.

(c) Greater creative education for those who do worship regularly so that their worship is no longer just a convention or habit judged by its quantity rather than its quality. In the many ways suggested here – through understanding the nature of proclamation and prophecy in preaching, the importance of symbolism, ceremonial and ritual to express

208

the many-sided feelings of human living, and the use of the
silence of 'being' rather than the frenzy of 'doing' – religious
worship could come alive. Then when we invite people to
'come to church' we would be inviting them to a communion, a being-with-others based on the fundamental
realities of human living which is also an incarnation of
divine depth. That is what worship is; anything else is a fake
and deserves the contempt and indifference which it gets.

1 Robin Green, *Only Connect* (Darton, Longman and Todd 1987),
  p. 1.
2 Charles Reich, *Greening of America* (Allen Lane 1971), pp. 211,
  212.
3 John V. Taylor, *The Go-Between God* (SCM Press 1972), pp. 148,
  149.
4 Robin Green, op. cit., p. 8.
5 Martin Buber, *Hasidism* (Philosophical Library 1948), p. 32.
6 Jurgen Moltmann, *Theology and Joy* (SCM Press 1973), p. 86.
7 Don Cupitt, *Radicals and the Future of the Church* (SCM Press
  1989), pp. 243, 245.
8 Paul Tillich, *The Shaking of the Foundations* (Penguin 1962),
  pp. 69, 70.
9 John V. Taylor, op. cit., p. 149.
10 Robin Green, op. cit., p. 120.
11 Kenneth Leech, *Care and Conflict* (Darton, Longman and Todd
  1990), pp. 79, 85.
12 Kahlil Gibran, *The Prophet* (Heinemann 1926), p. 94.
13 Don Cupitt, op. cit., pp. 170, 171.
14 R.S. Thomas, 'The Possession', *Later Poems 1972–1982*, Macmillan 1983.
15 James Joyce, *Portrait of the Artist as a Young Man* (Penguin 1969)
  p. 143.
16 Samuel Miller, *The Great Realities* (Longman Green 1956), p. 89.
17 Robin Green, op. cit., p. 56.

26

FUTURE DEVELOPMENT IN PERSONAL SPIRITUALITY

I come now to the last chapter of this book. It is perhaps the most difficult one, since spirituality is such an all-embracing theme of living that it cannot be separated from the other sections of this book. Spirituality covers all in life that is seeking to develop value, meaning, reality – the Way, the Truth, the Life of which Jesus speaks. Theology, sexuality, community, structure, training and worship are all concerned with our spirituality.

Perhaps spirituality is best defined in the words of St Paul, that we should be growing towards mature humanity 'measured by nothing less than the full stature of Christ... Bonded and knit together by every constituent part, the whole frame grows through the due activity of each part and builds itself up in love' (Ephesians 4:13,16). Paul speaks of the whole church, but it could equally well be the way by which we measure our own personal growth in spirituality. Many very valuable books have been written on spirituality, notably Kenneth Leech's *True God*[1] and Gerard Hughes's *God of Surprises*,[2] both of which I would commend strongly.

So what is left for me to say? Simply, in line with the general purposes of this book and its theme (namely, to pursue reality in every sphere of life – in theology, sexuality, community, structure and worship) to consider finally the task of the church to help each one of us in our personal experience of the spirit within: searching for meaning in our lives, working out the relationship between life and prayer, and trying to make sense of what it is we are looking for when we look within. In a world as frenzied and dissi-

210

pated in thinking as ours the need for contemplation becomes even greater, also for a deeper understanding of the different spiritual needs of the changing ages of life. It is to these matters that I would address myself since, despite the many profound books on spirituality, very little of their teaching seems to have permeated through normal teaching and training in local churches. Little is done there to help the average Christian relate her or his inner life of prayer and search for meaning to the realities of contemporary life.

I wrote in chapter 14 of how prayer as contemplation requires a capacity to concentrate and how the pressures of our society diminish that capacity. Think of the value, not only in personal spirituality but in understanding of meaning and the truth of our lives and the world, if churches were to plan their week to include help in training the congregation in the capacity to concentrate, to reflect, to be still and know God, ourselves and the world in which we live. It could help us to minimise violence by learning to understand and control our feelings. It could help to diminish the power of TV and the tabloid press to inflame gut-reaction. It could mean development within ourselves of the desire and capacity to know others at a deeper level and so learn what love truly means. It could also be the way by which God, the ground of our being, helps us from within to discover the truth about himself and to answer many other questions which our inward self is asking. St John of the Cross emphasises this as a result of contemplation:

> When the spirit is recollected and absorbed very attentively in some meditation, and in its reflection upon that same matter in its thinking, it proceeds from one stage to another, forming words and arguments which are very much to the point, with greater facility and distinctness and by means of its reasoning discovers things which it knew not with respect to the subject of its reflections, so that it seems not to be doing this itself, but rather it seems that another person is supplying the reasoning within its mind or answering its questions or teaching it.[3]

The value of reflection is also the subject of a poem by
D. H. Lawrence:

> Thought, I love thought,
> But not the jiggling and twisting of already existent ideas.
> I despise that self-important game.
> Thought is the welling up of unknown life into
>   consciousness,
> Thought is the testing of statements on the touchstone
>   of conscience,
> Thought is gazing on the face of life, and reading what
>   can be read,
> Thought is pondering over experience, and coming to a
>   conclusion,
> Thought is not a trick, or an exercise, or a set of dodges,
> Thought is a man in his wholeness wholly attending.[4]

'A man in his wholeness wholly attending' – that is as
good a description of contemplation as could be. One would
have thought that trying to help human beings to reach that
wholeness of attention to life and reality would be amongst
the first priorities of parish life, but in my experience that
is far from the case. How then should the church of the
future be working to achieve that wholeness amongst its
members and encourage their growth in spirituality?

I see this taking four forms: (1) training, especially among
the young, in the use of silence and in increasing their
powers of concentration; (2) group training in contemplation; (3) developing intercessory prayer; (4) developing
forms of spirituality relevant to each age-group.

1. TRAINING IN SILENCE AND CONCENTRATION

First it will be necessary to see that all early education of
children and young people contains training in the use
of silence and concentration. Some will say that to train
young people to be still and reflect is impossible, but in my
own teaching experience I have found that this is not so.
Stillness communicates itself, and by use of suitable music

(as has been discovered at Taizé) a very reflective atmosphere can be obtained amongst large crowds of young people.

For young and older people the first lesson to learn is the use of the body: the most relaxed and yet attentive way to sit (usually with hands gently on knees and feet firmly on the floor, in a chair which is upright but comfortable); then, with body alert, to learn the art of concentration by reflecting upon a single word or sentence and jotting down on paper the results of such reflection; then to extend that to a paragraph from a newspaper and reflect on what that paragraph is saying about life, its problems and difficulties, its joys and celebrations. This is exactly what Lawrence means when he says 'gazing on the face of life and reading what can be read'.

Breathing is also important to contemplation; we are, of course, always breathing but we do not often make ourselves deliberately conscious of our breathing. If we attend to our breathing in and breathing out we begin to experience a rhythm of life which helps us to be still and enter into the depths of ourselves.

Dealing with noise is also important. It is sometimes thought that noise is destructive of concentration, but it need not be so. Many young people have learnt how to deal with noise. I know many who almost need noise as an aid to concentration – for example, music as a background to homework and study. I am not one of those myself by nature but I have trained myself and others to deal with noise, not by shutting it out but by absorption. One can learn to do this when sitting in a bus or underground train. First listen quite deliberately to the outside noises. Usually we tend to think of the outside noises as getting in the way, but if we deliberately take them in they become a part of life and we, as it were, concentrate through them – they become almost a help as they form a background to the life we are seeking in its meaning. The noise of traffic is a murmur of humankind. I remember when I was at Camberwell I used to go into the youth club with its disco and be able, just because the noise of the disco prevented any one-to-one communication, to find a silence of thought through the noise. Do not misunderstand me. I am not advocating noise. I am saying it is possible for people to be trained to take noise into their system and so reach the silence which is at the heart of our being and that of God through it.

2. GROUP TRAINING IN CONTEMPLATION

Once the basic art of concentration has been learned, the work of concentration can then be extended. I would suggest that every parish should have what is often called a 'Julian cell' (I would not use that name in the inner city, but call it an experiment with depth or 'life below the surface'). I would publicise it as a means of seeking to know what lies beneath the surface of living. In such cells the threefold use of body, mind and spirit would be taught as the promotion of that harmony which can use silence and be a means of promoting reflection and concentration at the deeper levels of life. One of the most important results of the influence of Eastern mysticism, especially yoga, is that at long last the Western world is beginning to realise what the East has long known – the effect the body has upon our capacity for concentration and reflection. We should have always known this, for it is mentioned in the Book of Wisdom: 'For a perishable body weighs down the soul, and this earthly tent burdens the thoughtful mind' (Wisdom 9:15).

We all know what a difference it makes to our concentration, and therefore our prayer and contemplation, if we are tired, aching, too cold or too hot; it also makes a great difference if our body is alert and fit. Lack of exercise and use of the body, over-feeding or drinking, imposing unnecessary stress, all these have not only an effect upon our physical but also our spiritual well-being. Improved posture, exercises, conscious breathing can all help the redemption of the body and so make it one with the mind and spirit in the search for reality. Some of us have learned, through the teachings of Father Slade at the Anchor Hold and of others, how to use movement and dance as acts of prayer and reflection on living. Father Dechanet in his book *Christian*

214

Yoga gives many valuable exercises to help the body relate to the mind and spirit, and I would strongly recommend his book. He explains the relationship between body and spirituality better than I can:

> If certain ways of holding the body, certain attitudes and physical exercises by their nature bring myself into harmony with God and make it easier to receive graces, here is a practical example of how the body is redeemed.[5]

Then by the use of simple words or phrases the members of the cell would be led to the art of concentrating the mind in the same way as exercises have led to concentration in the body. The famous fourteenth-century treatise, *The Cloud of Unknowing*, explains the method:

> A naked intention directed to God, and to himself alone, is wholly sufficient. If you want this intention summed up in a word, to retain it more easily, take a short word, preferably of one syllable, to do so. The shorter the word the better, being more like the working of the Spirit. A word like 'GOD' or 'LOVE' . . . And fix this word fast to your heart, so that it is always there come what may . . . With this word you will hammer the cloud and the darkness above you.[6]

3. INTERCESSORY PRAYER

In chapter 14 I wrote also of the inadequacy of much intercessory prayer; I think the church has to rethink its teaching about intercessory prayer. We have to understand, as I have said earlier, that the love of God does not mean the removal or even the healing of pain and suffering but rather the sharing of pain and a willingness to enter ourselves into the suffering of others; the sharing is both Christ's (hence the crucifixion) and ours. Prayer then becomes not so much an appeal to the omnipotence of God to change things which by their nature are not likely to be changed, as a willingness to hold people and events persistently and without fail before the context of our faith, within our conviction that all life, here and hereafter, matters and that love is at the heart of life. If I do not believe that, then obviously all talk of God would be the nonsense that atheists allege, but equally there would be no point in any shared quiet holding of others before the Being of all life and the solidarity of all life.

A former Dean of St Paul's, Alan Webster, spoke of an old friend who wrote to him saying, 'I am beginning to believe more and more about less and less.' That is the condition of many. To put before them beliefs about the results of prayer which they find do not happen is only to provoke disbelief and disillusion and pain. Rather should we have just one belief, that the ground of all being is creative love and that creative love is seen in the interdependence of all things in creation, the unity and solidarity which lies behind all life if it is to continue to exist. Then, in the context of that belief, we may come to see how closely linked are absence and presence. Jesus' cry on the cross, 'My God, my God, why have you forsaken me?' (his experience of the absence of God) is followed by 'Father, into thy hands I commend my spirit' (a prayer of confidence in the presence of God).

It is because I believe in the reality of the presence that I can hold all who need the presence before the apparent absence. What the short-term results will be I do not know and cannot know, but I do not give up; I continue to name people and events before the one I call God. I know that I am in some way furthering the purposes of that creative love without which life could not continue, and that in some way which I cannot see, the purposes of love are being served. Without too much probing into exact results we can echo the words of Mother Julian:

> He shall make well all that is not well. How it shall be done there is no creature beneath Christ that knoweth it nor shall know it until it is done . . . All shall be well, and all shall be well, and all manner of things shall be well.[7]

It is to be noted that Mother Julian admits that no one

knows how God works but is confident because of his nature that all shall be well.

That is the way in which I hope intercession will be taught in the church of the future. In this way a great deal of the unreality of prayer would be taken away and we would not have to be so concerned about the absence of God. Sometimes, as we find in our own deepest relationships, the reality of the loved one who is absent is greater than that of many who are present with us daily, as Sartre once wrote while waiting for a friend in a café, 'My friend who was absent was more present than all the people who were there.'

There is need too to learn the value of being alone for, however close we are to someone else, we are in fact always alone and we have to end life alone. It is in our aloneness that we ask our questions of God, of truth, of justice, of relationship with others, and the very fact of coping with these questions enables us to be of more service to others who are alone. As Dag Hammarskjöld so rightly said: 'What makes loneliness an anguish is not that I have no one to share my burden, but this: I have only my own burden to bear.'[8] Dr Hobson, a psychiatrist in Manchester, says in a paper on 'Loneliness':

> ... the word 'alone' carries overtones and undertones of 'all-one'. I now catch glimpses of what it might mean to say 'I am myself', a myself which is an ideal wholeness embracing togetherness with another, with all others ... and yet perhaps with all nature. I am distinct and differentiated. Yet I am integrated in all relationships. Growing up involves the progressive achievement of a capacity to be alone and to be together with others. Aloneness and togetherness are interdependent. I can only be alone in so far as I can be together with others. I can only be together with others if I am able to be alone.[9]

There is especially need these days, when so many people live alone – single and divorced people of all ages as well as those who have been widowed – to help the lonely to find fulfilment in aloneness. But how can I help others to be alone if I know nothing of the suffering of loneliness and the joy of aloneness, and the difference between the two? When I knew that God had called me by nature to be a bachelor, I knew that there were only three possibilities open to me: either to find another like myself to share my life, but that was unlikely owing to the difficulties which the church would have made by their disapproval; to join a religious community, but that would have meant taking vows which I did not feel convinced were meant for me; or to live alone. So I was, like many others, called to the reality, in both the sadness and the joy, of aloneness. In this reality I was greatly helped by knowing that Christ had shared it with me.

4. SPIRITUALITY FOR EACH AGE-GROUP

The third reality with which I would deal is that of helping every age-group to develop the spirituality appropriate to it. The young, the middle-aged, the old, all have a creative contribution to make to society, and by so doing help themselves to continue to be of worth at each stage of life.

At present in the Western world there is an inappropriate lack of balance in attitudes towards the different age-groups. There is a foolish adulation of youth: in many areas of business and professional life the age at which employees are considered 'too old' gets younger and younger; advertising centres on the different ways in which one can preserve outward physical youth. In our Western world the older we get, the less worth we have in the eyes of society. The aim of Christian spirituality should be to see all age-groups as having their own unique contribution to make; these are not in competition but are complementary to each other.

The churches in the West have not been helpful in developing a balanced spirituality. Work with young people has all too often consisted simply in the provision of social and recreational clubs, discos and the like which, while they have their place, do little in themselves to develop creative values for living. Or else, as in some charismatic groups, there has been considerable emphasis on young communities with much valuable stress on community spirit but little on intellectual vigour and that questioning search which should be natural to the young. Work with middle-aged women has been more realistic, since many of the organisations such as the Mothers Union and women's fellowships do give some time to the consideration of the promotion of creative interests and the maturing of family life, but work with middle-aged men is almost non-existent. And as for older people there is all too often a rather patronising and 'do-gooding' attitude which provides Darby and Joan clubs and bingo sessions but does little to see older people as having a culture and spirituality which is creative and significant.

If we think of spirituality as the training in personal maturity by which body, mind and spirit are being developed to their full potential (and I can think of no better definition of spirituality), then it is obvious that there is no one pattern which is equally applicable at all stages of life. Spirituality must contain awareness of self, awareness of others and awareness of God, and these areas of awareness will take different forms at different times of life.

(a) Spirituality for the young

What then does self-awareness tell me about my youth? There will be a freshness and natural vigour in life and an intensity of emotion, because these are the realities of being young. As normally there will be many years in front of me I shall naturally be constantly looking to the future, having expectations of what it will hold for me in terms of success both in work and human relationships. I shall be much more aware of an interest in the future than in the past and therefore likely to be wanting to cast off what often appear to be shackles put upon me by parents and those in society brought up in a previous age. I shall often be painfully aware of my frustrations and inadequacies and yet be equally conscious of my impatience with those who try to control me; this will often make me appear on the one hand to be very self-conscious and embarrassed with others and at the same time frequently rude and arrogant as a form of self-defensiveness.

Human relationships are now for many young people a potential mine-field: sexual intimacy at the beginning of a relationship is far more common than in the past, but now any kind of promiscuity is threatened by AIDS. The knowledge that many have gained from the experience of their parents and from the world around them that marriage is not likely to be permanent leads many of them to shun the commitments of marriage and prefer to live with another with no binding promise of permanent commitment. This certainly avoids the dishonesty of serial marriage, when promises and vows are made over and over again only to be broken a few years later. When two young people live together with commitment to neither children nor marriage they are saying, 'We are aware of the fragility of relationship and we are only committing ourselves to the present and immediate future – we are living from day to day.' There is a certain biblical attitude here of 'letting the morrow take care of itself', but the risk is that great strain is put upon the continuation of the present if there are no other strengthening responsibilities, and the person's life is likely to become a constant series of changes. So here there is a tension between the natural looking to the future of which I have spoken and the equally strong desire to live in the present.

Other features of youth culture include a strong sense of community and a natural tendency to want to shock and rebel, often with violence. Both can have their negative and positive sides: negatively, the community sense often becomes little more than a herd instinct to follow the dress, customs and addictions of peers in such matters as drugs and gang violence; positively, in a willingness often to demonstrate for causes, fast in aid of famine relief and give enthusiastic support to such efforts for the starving as Bob Geldorf has made. Youth is a time for hero-worship, but it may be for a Terry Waite or a Sid Vicious. It is a time for ideals and rebellion, but the idealist may degenerate into the upwardly mobile 'yuppie' – their ideal being the initiative and the degeneration being the selfish absorption in a material consumerism. The rebellion may be for justice, peace and freedom, expressed in marches and community work, or it may take the form of a self-conscious desire to shock, as exhibited by many of the current Rock groups, promoting sexual violence and racism, such as America's young 'black rappers'.

Many of the attitudes of young people are those we would expect from a generation partly leaving and partly clinging to the safety and dependence of childhood and yet wanting to find a grown-up identity, but not yet quite sure what that is. Carl Jung aptly summarises this:

> If we try to extract the common and essential factors from the almost inexhaustible variety of individual problems found in the period of youth, we meet in nearly all cases with a particular feature: a more or less patent clinging to the childhood level of consciousness – a rebellion against the fateful forces in and around us which tend to involve us in the world. Something in us wishes to remain a child; to be unconscious, or, at most, only conscious of the ego; to reject everything foreign, or at least subject it to our will; to do nothing, or else to indulge our own craving for pleasure or power.[10]

The church's contribution to the spirituality of the young will be to be aware of these various attributes of that period of life and to make opportunities for their creative development. It should not be difficult for opportunities to be found both locally and nationally which can engage the idealistic tendencies of young people and engage those tendencies in practical work: for example, in many of the Green issues; in the promotion of community work especially for the aged; in forming groups to keep an eye on local problems which need tackling by organised lobbying, demonstrations, letters to the press, etc. Concerts could be promoted which would not only engage the talents and initiative of the young but also be for a cause which would enlist their interest and enthusiasm. A proper sense of rebellion against stultifying ideas and unnecessary dogmatism and convention should be encouraged and the young be given as great a share in the preparation of ideas for worship and prayer and study groups as are the older members of the congregation; in fact it should be clearly understood in the parish that the life of the church is a shared life in which each age-group has its proper part, with no one group dominating over the others. In every part of the community, whether inside or outside that of the church, there should be a sharing of what each age-group has to offer in both ideas and activities, so that the compartmentalism often so much a feature of local life is broken down and people begin to understand and empathise with each other and contribute to, rather than stand apart from, each other. One excellent way of encouraging this is to arrange parish holidays in which young and older people go away together and learn what it is like to live and share with each other.

In whatever way it is done – whether through social life, study, thinking together, praying together – there should be the aim of seeking to promote that creative development which is the meaning of maturity. This means going along with what are the natural desires and attractions of youth, but guiding these so that they may contribute to the whole-ness, unity and maturity of themselves and society rather than to what is divisive and destructive. It is my experience that when this is wisely done, alongside and not imposed upon the young, good results will be found also in their personal relationships of life. When I was a young priest in the diocese of Chelmsford the youth chaplain, the Revd Sam Erskine, arranged a series of summer holidays for young people in which the needs of body, mind and spirit were catered for in recreation, thinking, prayer and worship. The community and relationships formed there had an influence for life on the maturity of those who came, as I saw when many years later I met again some of them, by then in their fifties and even sixties, and found that the creative spirituality learned all those years ago was still evident in their attitudes to life, to each other and to the church.

(b) Spirituality for the middle-aged

I begin here with another extract from Jung, as quoted by Christopher Bryant in *Jung and the Christian Way*:

The nearer we approach the middle of life and the

> better we have succeeded in entrenching ourselves in
> our personal attitudes and social positions, the more it
> appears as if we had discovered the right course and
> the right ideals and principles of behaviour. For this
> reason we suppose them to be eternally valid, and make
> a virtue of unchangeably clinging to them. We overlook
> the essential fact that the social goal is attained only
> at the cost of a diminution of personality.[11]

Jung has it exactly right. Middle age, if we are not careful,
becomes the time that we call 'settling down'. This 'settling
down' often means becoming quite incapable of entertain-
ing any ideas different from those we have adopted as our
own; we become 'stuck' in the prejudices, the social, political
and religious ideas we have decided are 'safe' and undisturbing and, what is worse, we often expect that everyone
else shall share those ideas, as if they are 'eternally valid'. It
is also often the period when materialism takes over and
when money and social position become our goals in life. In
most cases the result is political and religious conservatism, a
distaste for anyone or anything which is not what is called
'normal' and conventional, and a wish that our children
shall follow in our own footsteps of what we call 'success' in
the world.

On the other hand, there are present in this period of
life values which can be shaped into a more positive and
creative frame. The very fact that middle age has usually
become the time for family responsibilities and probably
the exercise of authority, and therefore accountability to
colleagues and work-mates as well as to the public, means
that awareness and sensitivity to others become more important than in youth. Maturity in this age-group consists in the
capacity to be aware of and to further the potentialities of
those around us, whether at home or at work. It also means
that, when Jesus said that the Holy Spirit would guide us
into all truth, he did not mean 'but only until I am forty-
five for by then I shall have learnt it all'!

The task of the church then in this period of life is to be
aware of what will be the main difficulties encountered and
to help to ease men and women through these difficulties,

also to encourage the development of aspects of life other than simply money-getting and status.

There are particular features and difficulties of this period of life:

(i) This is the time when young people leave home and begin their independent lives. Husband and wife will be left alone together without the bonding of other family members. If the marriage has lost its freshness and if communication has become stale between them, this will be a very dangerous period for their relationship. A church which spends much time talking about the family and the importance of lasting relationships should stop being sentimental and face realistically the difficulties of married life. Members of the church should be encouraged within a supportive atmosphere to share openly those difficulties, and married couples might well be taught to pray them out together in joint prayers.

(ii) Stress is more likely to occur at this period of life than at any other, and may be occasioned by different factors: holding one's job in a time of recession and redundancy; anxiety about health and getting older (the stress illnesses of obesity, breakdown, heart attacks, strokes are probably at their greatest in the fifties to sixties); family difficulties, on the one hand with elderly parents and their care and on the other with getting used to the son-in-law or daughter-in-law introduced into the family and not always the choice one would have wished for.

Spiritual help will be needed, both practical and psychological, if the apparent failure and rejection of unemployment has to be faced. There need to be in the church some people who are trained as counsellors and are available as listening ears when stress needs release; prayer also should be taught as a means of release, to be able to pour out upon God frustration, anger, resentment – all the feelings which only fester if bottled up. Jesus' words, 'Come unto me all you who are heavy-laden' are meant as an invitation to unload stress upon God. Practical support and sharing are also needed when there are family difficulties – 'granny-sitting' may be even more important than 'baby-sitting'!

More attention needs to be given to that alliance of the spiritual to the physical which diminishes the risk of psychosomatic illness: the cultivation of relaxation of both body and mind by meditation; exercises at the beginning of the day; a daily rest and daily walk; moderation in eating and drinking and choosing the right kind of food; the choice of a kind of holiday that will be truly relaxing and the special qualities of spiritual and mental refreshment offered by an annual retreat. All of these should be part of the programme of a church which is aware of the spiritual needs of the middle-aged.

(iii) This is also the time when preparation can begin for the promotion of cultural and spiritual interests which will carry over into the later periods of life. Jung, while realising that the morning of adult life has to be given over to the care of children and family and the earning of money, is insistent that these values are not for ever to take priority:

> Whoever carries over into the afternoon the law of the morning, or the natural aim, must pay for it with damage to his soul, just as surely as a growing youth who tries to carry over his childish egoism into adult life must pay for this mistake with social failure. Money-making, social achievement, family and posterity are nothing but plain *nature*, not *culture*. Culture lies outside the purpose of nature. Could by any chance culture be the meaning and purpose of the second half of life?

And Bryant adds: 'Culture . . . everything that broadens the mind and uplifts the spirit, everything that gives a transcendent meaning to life and especially religion'.[12]

This is very true: in my experience some of the most pathetic examples of retirement have been those of business executives who gave all their life and interests to the promotion of business and money-making. When it came to retirement they had no other interests, became bored, and often death or senility followed. Middle age is the time to enlarge cultural interests, to find other avenues than money-making to engage the mind and spirit, to make new searchings for truth so that the mind and soul is ever awake to new revelations and does not get stuck in that wooden intransigence and dull conformity which is so oppressive to family, neighbours and local church. Sadly and all too often the local church colludes with the lower levels of being which bar the way to further understanding and questioning, and in the thinking and preaching there is a sad mixture of simplistic, childish beliefs (not in the true sense of 'becoming as children' in trust, but rather in credulity) and a conservatism which actually tries to stop any new understanding of belief or spirituality.

Schumacher says that human beings should continually be seeking higher levels of being since ' . . . the higher the level of being, the greater, richer and more wonderful is the world . . . and the higher the level of being the less is the fixity and the greater the plasticity of nature'. If we do not move on to these higher levels of being then:

> . . . the higher powers of man, no longer brought into play to produce the knowledge of wisdom, atrophy and even disappear altogether. As a result, all problems that society or individuals are called upon to tackle become insoluble . . . While wealth may still be accumulating, the quality of man declines.[13]

The task of the church then will be to encourage, not discourage, the questioning of faith and society, so that we can ever move to higher levels of understanding of truth, and not only help the world around us but also develop our own interests and stretch our faculties of thinking.

In the parish where I live a class is being led by a retired priest, a considerable scholar, into the background of the books of the Bible. Many of those attending show, from their questions and sometimes even disturbance, that they have never before delved into the background of the book which alone gives them the knowledge of their very faith. Yet all of these people have been 'successful' in the world and have been Christians all their lives. Why has that broadening of the mind and spirit on the source of their beliefs never been available to them until now? The most important and continual training in the church should surely be, through study groups and research, the enlargement of the mind and spirit which is true spirituality.

(c) Spirituality for the old

The reality of old age is not a declining reality but a different reality. We have been talking about the different periods of life, each of which has its contribution to bring. There is a freshness and vitality in being young; there is maturity and stability in middle age; there is the contribution of wisdom and understanding of life which old age can and should bring. But people of each age will only live positively if they bring what is appropriate to their age. Just as young people can be anything but fresh and vital, and the middle-aged can be stuffy and conventional rather than mature, so old people are not necessarily wise. Some old people are always looking backwards, trying eternally to be young without knowing how; some are difficult, awkward, bad-tempered, almost impossibly demanding to live with. Society can be hopelessly unrealistic in dealing with the old, veering between denying them significance or worth, just because they are old, and humouring and pampering them, again just because they are old.

We need that positive outlook on age which is the theme of Browning's poem:

> Grow old along with me!
> The best is yet to be,
> The last of life, for which the first was made:
> Our times are in His hand
> Who saith, 'A whole I planned,
> Youth shows but half; trust God: see all, nor be afraid!'[14]

The Bible is quite realistic about old age, in both its negative and positive aspects. It does not hide the fact of physical deterioration, of the day 'when the keepers of the house shall tremble, and the strong men shall bow themselves, and the grinders cease because they are so few, and those that look out of the window be darkened' (Ecclesiastes 12:3–4 AV). But the Book of Job associates wisdom with old age: 'There is wisdom, remember, in age and long life brings understanding' (12:12). Also in Ecclesiasticus:

> How fine a thing sound judgement with grey hairs . . . how fine a thing wisdom in the aged and considered advice . . . the crown of old men is ripe experience, their true glory – the fear of the Lord . . . as the clear light upon the golden candlestick so is the beauty of the face in ripe old age (25:4–6; 26:17).

The writer of Ecclesiasticus is not talking about the beauty manufactured in beauty parlours or the usually vain attempts of an old sheep to look and dress like a lamb or the eternal adolescent of the club or male bar. Rather is he talking of the face which is already mirroring something of the eternal and the signs of resurrection. Baruch gives some good advice for the spirituality of the aged: ' . . . learn where is wisdom, where is strength, where is understanding: that thou mayest know also where is length of days and life, where is the light of the eyes and peace' (3:14).

The appropriate spirituality for the old is the continuation of the three aspects of culture already mentioned when thinking of the middle-aged: namely, the broadening of the mind, the uplifting of the spirit and the transcendental meaning to life which comes with facing the reality of death. Each one of these is to be developed in reaction to the particular difficulties of old age.

First then there will be continuation of the broadening of the mind and resistance to the tendency to look backwards. Jung again writes with truth: 'It is better to go forwards with the stream of time than backwards against it.'[15] Resistance to change and the tendency to be always comparing the past to the present, with the implication that the past was better, is very common in the elderly, and many a church has suffered from weak vicars who allow the backward-looking elderly to rule in their churches. If we are truly to help the old to a vital spirituality we have to resist this tendency and to enable them to find the truth of T. S. Eliot's saying 'Old men ought to be explorers.'[16] This is precisely what some of

our greatest old men and women have been: Pope John
XXIII, Bertrand Russell, Emmanuel Shinwell, Edith Evans,
the Queen Mother and Mother Teresa to name but a few.
What has made them as they are? Is it as Cicero has asserted:
'Old men preserve their intellect so long as they preserve
their interests'? Speaking for myself I am glad to say that I
have been more rather than less radical, both religiously
and politically, since the age of forty-five and I owe this to
the inspiration of the 1960s and to people like Bishop John
Robinson, Mervyn Stockwood, Eric James, Monica Furlong,
all of whom continued to think and to question. So if the
church wishes to develop the spirituality of the aged, let it
not encourage and give way to the temptation to look backwards and resist change but rather do everything it can in
the life and organisation of the local and national church
to encourage every one of us to go forwards with the stream
of time. I recall hearing it said that 'age does not depend
upon years but upon temperament and health. Some are
born old and some never grow old.' In our spirituality training we would do well to remember also the words of a poet:

> Age is a quality of mind.
> If you have left your dreams behind,
> If hope is cold:
> If you no longer look ahead,
> If your ambition's fires are dead,
> Then you are old.[17]

Secondly, there will be the uplifting of the spirit. Here
there is a work of education to be done, of the old themselves and more especially of the society which refuses to
see worth in age. This has, of course, nothing to do with the
Christian understanding of human beings nor that of other
religions. It is simply the product of a secular and capitalist
society which tends to measure people by their capacity to
be productive in monetary terms. Through the years of
Thatcherism we have developed a view of society in which
wealth-making takes priority over service to the community;
then, of course, when retirement comes and one's capacity
for wealth-making ceases, so also does one's value in society.

The Christian understanding of a human being assesses worth not on any criteria of wealth or of age but on inner value. The Jewish tradition of honour to the aged was a tradition common to all Orientals, and is so to this day; the Talmud says, 'Who is sure of heaven? He who honours the aged.' (By this standard few in Western society could be sure of heaven!)

So if there is to be an uplifting of the spirit for the old, there has to be a liberation theology for the old. By that I mean they have to be rescued from the ideology that labels them a subservient group to be grateful for the provision of services, health and personal care – services which they have not only in most cases already paid for but have a right to expect. There should be liberation from the Darby and Joan, 'silver threads amongst the gold' syndrome – the dear old things who have to be looked after with tea and bingo, an attitude which is both demeaning and non-creative for them and society. We need a profound change in attitude towards the old, by society as represented through welfare services and by the church, a change which is free from sentimentality and of rejection as being no longer significant.

There are various ways in which churches can help to free the elderly from their oppression by supporting them in that uplifting of the spirit which comes from consciousness of worth and rights:

(i) The new pensioners, being more sophisticated than previously, are beginning to recognise that they have rights and are learning how to take action to maintain and increase them. By the sheer increasing weight of numbers the senior citizens are now a powerful influence in society and their 'lobby' has to be heeded by politicians. I hope that future social services and the church will gear their work with the elderly more towards training them to be politically conscious and away from the tea-and-bingo-type club, so that they will know their worth, refuse to be ignored and learn how to contribute the experience they have to the welfare of society.

(ii) There is a deeper sense in which we learn to value our worth in relation to the other side of retirement –

the realisation that, while senior citizens should fight in the world for recognition of worth and rights, there is also the understanding that the glory of God in human beings is revealed by true passivity as well as by activity, the passivity which is very different from that of the Darby and Joan syndrome. W. H. Vanstone says that persons are as much human when receivers as they are when achievers.[18]

The gospels tell us how Jesus at a certain point in his ministry exchanged the active ministry for the passive: the God of love in Jesus came to the point of total exposure and helplessness, vulnerable, waiting, receiving – the ministry of the passion. Perhaps in this ministry the ultimate dimensions of God's glory were even more clearly seen than in his activity and achievement. This has come to me many times when visiting old people, now laid aside from active endeavour but who have seen this not as a sign of worthlessness or insignificance but as a sign of sharing in the passion of Christ. The pain of being laid aside from activity in old age seems to meet two different kinds of response: either resentment, querulous demands from others and from God, or a kind of dignity and acceptance which increases rather than diminishes the stature of old age. Just as Christ lets himself into the pain of the world, so does this kind of passivity. Gerard Hughes expresses this: 'If we enter into the passion of Christ we begin to feel the pain of this world as Christ did, and his spirit at work in us takes this pain, absorbs it, and answers it with forgiveness and love.'[19] The worth that then comes from the senior citizen is a more powerful witness than many of our Christian activities. It is this worth that, by prayer and support, the people of the church, clergy and laity, should be constantly building up both in themselves and for others.

(iii) There is every reason why the elderly have much to offer society. To them alone belongs experience of every age of life, to them has been given experience of the joys and the difficulties of each age, the capacity to survive, stability and productivity in many areas of work, family and neighbourhood. The only time the old have little or nothing to offer is when they have become stuck at an earlier stage in life, so that in older age they simply reveal the childishness and irresponsibility of youth or the acquisitiveness and egoism of middle age.

Thirdly, there is the facing of the transcendental meaning of life which comes with the aloneness of old age and the facing of death. The aloneness of old age is almost inevitable, since rarely do couples die together. I wrote earlier in this chapter about the value of being alone, and especially in old age there is need for a spirituality which transforms loneliness into aloneness.

Every Christian group should give a high priority to the training which enables a person in later life to be alone. In our own old age we can offer, in our prayers and in our relationship to others, the experience of BEING rather than DOING. Our prayers may take the more contemplative form, more a waiting on God which will allow our neglected passive side to rise into consciousness and enrich and deepen us, and through us to enrich others also. The service we shall have to offer will be a service of being – we can be available for listening and counselling. This capacity just to be with others is very valuable in this complicated and pressurising world, and we shall find ourselves much in demand – in fact more in demand if we learn to *be* than if we are so over-active that we have little time for others.

The final training in the transcendental is in how to meet death. This has not been given the priority it should have had in the everyday life of the church. It is not sufficient just occasionally to preach about death. Since death is the one fact of life that each person knows will happen, it is the most real fact of life. Therefore, like everything else in life, it must be faced realistically, and if the church cannot help us in this most important finality of life, then what use is the church? How then should death be prepared for? Here I again refer to the words of Jung, as quoted in Bryant's book:

> I have observed that a life directed to an aim is in general better, richer, healthier than an aimless one . . .
> To a psychotherapist an old man who cannot bid fare-

well to life appears as feeble and as sickly as a young man who is unable to embrace it ... As a doctor I am convinced that it is hygienic ... to discover in death a goal towards which one can strive, that shrinking away from it is something unhealthy and abnormal, which robs the second half of life of its purpose.[20]

So it is the function of the church to help people to strive towards this goal in various ways:

(i) There should be practical preparation for death so that those who have to make arrangements when death has occurred will know what is the wish of the deceased. This will be in two respects: materially and financially in regard to the will (how many clergy actually do obey the Prayer Book by asking a very ill person, when visiting, if their affairs are in order?); also spiritually. I believe it is important to draw up one's own funeral service; it is a great help to the bereaved to know that their arrangements are as the deceased would wish.

(ii) There should be regular teaching and discussion about the reality of death and what it means to prepare for eternal life. The whole of life is life through death, and preparation for eternity is the way we live now. I have not seen it expressed better than by Bishop John Robinson when facing his own death:

> For the Christian, preparing for eternal life means real living, more abundant life, which is begun, continued through, not ended now. And this means it is about quality of life not quantity. How long it goes on here is purely secondary. So preparing for eternity means really learning to live, not just concentrating on keeping alive. It means living it up, becoming more concerned with contributing to and enjoying what matters most – giving the most to life and getting the most from it, while it is on offer.[21]

All life is a mixture of living and dying, and it is the capacity to let go in life, to risk the unknown, the unfamiliar, the disturbing, that enables new life to be born. The really dangerous temptation of old age is the desire to hang on to the familiar. So if encouragement is given to an attitude to life that says, 'Let be . . . let go . . . let God,' then death will simply be the last letting go and letting be. Dying in all events of life is the dark fact of coming alive, as each one of the disciples experienced in Christ's crucifixion and resurrection.

(iii) Let there be assurance in our teaching of life through death. The eternal is not fixed; it is simply the positive belief that there is no reason for an arbitrary ending to life. To quote Jung again:

> When I live in a house which I know will fall about my head within the next two weeks all my vital functions will be impaired by this thought; but if on the contrary I feel safe, I can dwell there in a normal and comfortable way . . . it would therefore be desirable to think of death as only a transition, as part of a life process whose extent and duration are beyond our knowledge.[22]

To me the belief in God and in eternal life are inseparable. If God is eternal then I must be also. If there is no eternity there can be no God, for it would be equally ridiculous to believe in a God who also died or in a God who lived on in some vague eternity with no one else and nothing there.

(iv) Finally, let the teaching of the church be clear and made known as to the *ritual* of dying – provided, of course, there is consciousness to the end. There should be a last confession and absolution, a last anointing and communion, preferably with family and friends, and then those final great words of commendation, 'Go forth into your world O Christian soul, etc.' My father had this kind of death. Somehow he knew the day of his death; we had communion and readings and absolution with all of us around him. It is not every death that can be as complete in ritual form as that, but it is good that we should at least tell our relatives and friends that that is what we want if conditions make it possible. And we should be able in those last days to talk with each other, openly, of the reality of death but equally with every assurance of the reality of eternal life.

The spirituality of old age is finely expressed in the following poem:

> I would grow lovely growing old
>> So many fine things to do.
>
> Laces and ivory and gold
>> and silks need not be new.
>
> There is healing in old trees.
> There is body in old wine.
> Old streets a glamour hold.
> Why may not I, as well as these,
>> Grow lovely growing old?[23]

To which I reply – why not indeed?

1 Kenneth Leech, *True God*, Sheldon Press 1985.
2 Gerard Hughes, *God of Surprises*, Darton, Longman and Todd 1985.
3 St John of the Cross, *Ascent of Mount Carmel*, chapter 29.
4 D. H. Lawrence, 'Thought', from *The Complete Poems*, vol. 2, Heinemann 1964.
5 J. M. Dechanet, *Christian Yoga* (Burns and Oates 1960), pp. 83–4.
6 *The Cloud of Unknowing*, trans. C. Wolters (Penguin 1961), p. 69.
7 Mother Julian of Norwich, *Revelations of Divine Love*, stanza 32.
8 Dag Hammarskjöld, *Markings* (Faber 1964), p. 85.
9 R. F. Hobson, in a paper reprinted from *The Journal of Analytical Psychology*, vol. 19, no. 1, 1974.
10 C. G. Jung, as quoted in Christopher Bryant, *Jung and the Christian Way* (Darton, Longman and Todd 1983), p. 56.
11 Ibid., p. 58.
12 Ibid., p. 61.
13 E. F. Schumacher, *A Guide for the Perplexed* (Jonathan Cape 1977), p. 68.
14 Robert Browning, 'Rabbi ben Ezra'.
15 Jung, in Bryant, op. cit., p. 62.
16 T. S. Eliot, 'East Coker', *Four Quartets*, Faber 1944.
17 Edward Tuck, in V. Sly, *I Quote* (Lutterworth Press 1964), p. 6.
18 W. H. Vanstone, *The Stature of Waiting*, Darton, Longman and Todd 1982.

19 Gerard Hughes, op. cit., p. 130.
20 Jung, in Bryant, op. cit., p. 62.
21 John Robinson, quoted in an anthology *Dawn through our Darkness*, compiled by Giles Harcourt (Collins 1985), p. 82.
22 Jung, in Bryant, op. cit., p. 62.
23 Karle Wilson Baker, in *I Quote*.

EPILOGUE

I began with a quotation from T. S. Eliot. I shall end also with quotations from his poetry:

> Old men ought to be explorers.

> Time present and time past
> Are both perhaps present in time future,
> And time future contained in time past.[1]

I am certainly an old man in the age levels of life, but I have always been an explorer theologically, ethically and politically, and hope I shall be to the end of my days. This book has been an exploration, as I see it, of time future for the church based upon my experience of time past and time present in my own life and ministry.

In Lewis Carroll's book *Alice through the Looking Glass*, Alice steps through the looking glass into a different world which in many ways is the reverse of the present world. My hope and vision is that time future for the church will in many ways reverse the attitudes of the present. I hope for a church where theology will be a continuing search for truth rather than hemmed in by the tramlines of evangelical fundamentalism and catholic tradition; when sexual ethics will be concerned with promoting the maximum wholeness of body, mind and spirit within whatever sexual orientation or circumstances have been given; when ministry, whether ordained or lay, will be based upon need, vocation and capacity rather than upon male domination and structural rigidity of function and gender; when the power of the church will be determined from below to above, from laity to bishop rather than the reverse; when the training of both clergy and laity will be undertaken together for the practical application of a community of love, the text of the Gospel in the context of society, and the promotion of the kingdom of God; when worship will be geared primarily neither to churchmanship nor to liturgical form but to the needs of small and large groups coming together to express solidarity of thought and feeling; and, finally, when training in personal spirituality will involve help in contemplative concentration, the understanding of how to address an apparently absent God in prayer and the spiritual needs of each age of life.

I am not convinced that Christ ever intended to create an institutionalised church; that came later with the growth of Christianity and its collusion with the power structures of society. But I am convinced that the vision of the future church which I have is in accord with the mind of Christ as I understand the proclamation of the kingdom which he made and that, unless we all work towards that vision of time future, the influence of the church will slowly become less and less in the structures of the world. David Jenkins, Bishop of Durham, has said: 'God is as he is in Jesus and therefore we have hope.' If we are to have hope for the future of the church it also must bear more clearly than at present the marks of Jesus.

1 T. S. Eliot, 'East Coker' and 'Burnt Norton', *Four Quartets*, Faber 1944.